The Diary of a Young Girl

'Fifty years have passed since Anne Frank's diary was first published. Her story came to symbolize not only the travails of the Holocaust, but the struggle of the human spirit in adversity ... Bergen-Belsen was liberated by British troops in April 1945. One of them wrote to me recently: "I was too late to save Anne Frank." That shows the impact that her story has made, and will continue to make. This edition is a worthy memorial'
Martin Gilbert, *The Times*

'A monument to the human spirit'
Phillip Knightley, *Mail on Sunday*

'This edition will shine a new light on Anne Frank for those who have read the original diary. And for readers new to her, including young people who are the age she was when she started writing, it will be an immensely powerful and enjoyable introduction to the multi-faceted person that she was and the world that she inhabited'
Reva Klein, *The Times Educational Supplement*

'Susan Massotty captures Anne's innocent cockiness, her sense of fun, the sweetness of the lonely adolescent ... There are a lot of lessons to be learnt from reading this beautiful book'
Gaia Servadio, *Observer*

'A witty, funny and tragic book ... Anne's gift, her early death, her Jewishness, are tailormade for the sainthood. The miracle is her diary. It flourished in the shadow of death, its author died at Belsen and yet it survived ... New version or old, this extraordinary book stands on its own even without its context of horror'
Silvia Rodgers, *Sunday Times*

Anne Frank was born on 12 June 1929. She died while imprisoned at Bergen-Belsen, three months short of her sixteenth birthday.

Otto H. Frank was the only member of his immediate family to survive the Holocaust. He died in 1980.

Mirjam Pressler is a popular, prize-winning writer of books for young readers and a well-known translator. She lives in Germany.

The translator, Susan Massotty, lives in Holland.

The Diary of a Young Girl

THE DEFINITIVE EDITION

Anne Frank

Edited by OTTO H. FRANK *and* MIRJAM PRESSLER
Translated by SUSAN MASSOTTY

With an introduction ELIE WIESEL,
translated by EUAN CAMERON

PENGUIN BOOKS

PENGUIN CLASSICS

Published by the Penguin Group
Penguin Books Ltd, 80 Strand, London WC2R ORL, England
Penguin Group (USA) Inc., 375 Hudson Street, New York, New York 10014, USA
Penguin Group (Canada), 90 Eglinton Avenue East, Suite 700, Toronto, Ontario, Canada M4P 2Y3
(a division of Pearson Penguin Canada Inc.)
Penguin Ireland, 25 St Stephen's Green, Dublin 2, Ireland (a division of Penguin Books Ltd)
Penguin Group (Australia), 250 Camberwell Road, Camberwell, Victoria 3124, Australia
(a division of Pearson Australia Group Pty Ltd)
Penguin Books India Pvt Ltd, 11 Community Centre, Panchsheel Park, New Delhi – 110 017, India
Penguin Group (NZ), 67 Apollo Drive, Rosedale, North Shore 0632, New Zealand
(a division of Pearson New Zealand Ltd)
Penguin Books (South Africa) (Pty) Ltd, 24 Sturdee Avenue,
Rosebank, Johannesburg 2196, South Africa

Penguin Books Ltd, Registered Offices: 80 Strand, London WC2R ORL, England

www.penguin.com

First published in the United States of America by Doubleday 1995
First published in Great Britain by Viking 1997
Published in Penguin Books 1997
Reprinted in Penguin Classics 2000

22

Copyright © The Anne Frank-Fonds, Basle, Switzerland, 1991
English translation copyright © Doubleday, a division of
Bantam Doubleday Dell Publishing Group, Inc., 1995
Introduction copyright © Elie Wiesel, 1997
Translation of the introduction copyright © Euan Cameron, 1997

Photographs copyright © The Anne Frank-Fonds, Basle, Switzerland;
Anne Frank Stichting
All rights reserved

The moral right of the copyright holders has been asserted

The translator is grateful to Stacy Knecht for her editorial assistance and to
Nancy Forest-Flier for her translation of the poems on pages 106–7, 150, 237

Printed in England by Clays Ltd, St Ives plc

978-0-141-18275-9
www.greenpenguin.co.uk

Contents

Introduction

On 12 June 1942, in an Amsterdam seized by uncertainty and terror, a young Jewish girl celebrates her thirteenth birthday by beginning a personal diary which, a few years after her death, would grip the emotions of millions of readers throughout the world.

Was it because Anne Frank was the witness to an age in which horror had become the norm rather than the exception? Did Anne Frank's severed life and destiny make her the symbol of a wounded generation, of a sacrificed race?

How can we explain the continuing influence of her diaries on both Jewish and non-Jewish readers alike? Is it the age of the author that so affects us? Her innocence perhaps? Other young people, her contemporaries, have described what they saw and experienced in the ghettos of Poland and Czechoslovakia. Hers is the only account to have captured and conquered the hearts and imagination of the wider public.

And yet ... The impact of the narrative is due as much to what lies within the book as to what is omitted. The true tragedy, so final and terrifying in the absolute totality of its dimensions, that of Auschwitz, only begins afterwards, that is to say, after the last page of this diary has been turned.

Is it because we already sense what is to happen? A

presence, like a thief in the night, waiting and watching. Hovering.

Like Death.

At the beginning of the book, Anne is the daughter of a middle-class family, still a child, on the threshold of adolescence. The Germans are already the masters of Holland, as well as of most of Europe, but her preoccupations are, one might say, astonishingly ordinary. The anti-Jewish laws irritate and upset her, but they do not frighten her. A curfew for Jews? Restricted freedom of movement? It's not too ghastly. No longer allowed to go for bicycle rides? She will walk. Forbidden to attend normal schools? Oh well, she'll enrol at the Jewish lycée. Anne discusses it all good-humouredly, quoting one of her girl-friends: 'I don't dare do anything anymore, 'cause I'm afraid it's not allowed.'

In late June 1942, Anne is longing for the summer holidays: 'One more week and our torment will be over.' Anne adores looking at herself in the mirror. She flirts with boys. She composes poetry that makes the whole class laugh. Meanwhile, in Warsaw the ghetto is being stifled. In Babi-yar, tens of thousands of corpses are already starting to decompose in communal graves.

Did this not show surprising *naïveté* in a family of Jewish refugees from Germany who should have conducted themselves with more awareness, greater perspicacity? In Hungary, up until the arrival of the Germans in the spring of 1944, the Jews had behaved in a similar fashion. We did not know. And Anne had only a vague idea.

It was not until 5 July 1942, when her elder sister Margot received a call-up notice from the SS, that their father, Otto Frank, decided that the time had come for his family and a few of their friends to go underground.

And it was only at this point in Anne's notebooks, when

she confides in her diary as if it were a real person by the name of Kitty, who has her own way of thinking, that the story takes on a different tone. She is no longer a child. It is as if she had changed not merely in attitude, but also in her expression . . . Her voice too. She retains her gaiety, but frequently, more than frequently, at the very core of her being, she slumps into a depression: she swallows valerian tablets to calm herself. She pays for each moment of joy with a fit of remorse, for she is reflecting silently on all those who, already driven from their homes, are suffering misfortune and misery.

In the ghetto that is the Annexe, the hiding-place where she and those dear to her are to remain incarcerated and isolated for over two years, a transformation begins to take place, a gradual and profound maturing process. All of a sudden, the over-sensitive and quarrelsome girl, unpredictable and full of drive and energy, blessed with a ferocious critical sense and a biting, occasionally pitiless, sense of humour, develops a precocious intelligence which, in other circumstances, would have seemed quite disconcerting.

All at once, everything interests her. Not just what is going on around her – the daily incidents, the problems of food and safety, the complex and changing relationships between the different members of the little community bound together by the same menace, her mother's incomprehension – but also the events that are taking place far from home: Hitler and Stalin, Lemberg and Stalingrad, the condition of women throughout history and the role of God in human affairs. On 9 October 1942, quoting the BBC, she refers to the Jews who, far away, were being sent to the gas chambers by the Germans. In March 1944, she alludes to the German occupation of Hungary. She wonders what will happen to the million Jews who still live there. She talks, she chats, she even reproaches herself for being a gossip. All she really loves to do is to write. Her dream is to become a journalist. And a writer. She describes her thoughts, she writes stories. But her main concern is to write about herself. And she does so with skill. Occasionally, one comes across a sentence that is painful, that is heart-rending. How can a girl of barely fourteen years of age have accumulated so much anger, so much wisdom, so much experience about the human condition?

At the same time, on an immediate and personal level, everything that happens in a normal environment is mirrored in the Annexe. In a more concentrated form. A speedy adaptation to a hidden, restricted life. The 'residents' are both separated and drawn together by feelings of jealousy and moderation, by selfish tendencies and generous impulses, by ambition and remorse. You could almost look upon it as a play; when Anne goes back to join Peter, with whom, to her great surprise, she has begun to fall in love, it is as if she were moving from one stage set to another: they have such plans, it's all a great adventure. Such a drama. Their love story is so touching, with its tentative, circumspect beginnings. The two lovers will die before they can discover the joy of its fulfilment.

But before that, there is the anxiety. Alongside the good, the 'protectors' who, at the risk of their lives, provide them with food, books and information from the outside world, there are the wicked, the informers, the Nazi collaborators. The fear of being discovered, of being arrested and deported.

Towards the end of 1943 and the beginning of 1944, events moved quickly. The Normandy landings. The intensification of the persecutions. Anne had premonitions. The noises from below, from the other side. The burglars. The arrests. When would it be their turn? She described all this in her diaries.

Suffering from loneliness in this atmosphere of forced proximity, she confides only in Kitty. Now, Kitty is ourselves, the reader. Ultimately, it is to us that she appeals. Almost as if she were making us trustees of her will.

She also mentions her dreams, her aspirations: to return to her lessons at school, to go to Switzerland, to breathe in fresh air, to become a mother. Death, at Bergen-Belsen, will obliterate them all: her future will be stolen from us.

But, at a certain moment, 11 November 1943, she loses her fountain pen to which she is very attached. She searches for it everywhere, to no avail. At this point, she pronounces this terrible sentence: 'I'm left with one consolation, small though it may be: my fountain pen was cremated, just as I would like to be some day.'

At Auschwitz she would have been. Her mother was. Peter too. So were the other residents of the Annexe. And millions of Jews. Only her father survived. And it is he who has passed this book down to us.

A book?

A wound.

ELIE WIESEL
Translated from the French by Euan Cameron

Foreword

Anne Frank kept a diary from 12 June 1942 to 1 August 1944. Initially, she wrote it strictly for herself. Then, one day in 1944, Gerrit Bolkestein, a member of the Dutch government in exile, announced in a radio broadcast from London that after the war he hoped to collect eyewitness accounts of the suffering of the Dutch people under the German occupation, which could be made available to the public. As an example, he specifically mentioned letters and diaries.

Impressed by this speech, Anne Frank decided that when the war was over she would publish a book based on her diary. She began rewriting and editing her diary, improving on the text, omitting passages she didn't think were interesting enough and adding others from memory. At the same time, she kept up her original diary. In the scholarly work *The Diary of Anne Frank: The Critical Edition* (1989), Anne's first, unedited diary is referred to as version *a*, to distinguish it from her second, edited diary, which is known as version *b*.

The last entry in Anne's diary is dated 1 August 1944. On 4 August 1944, the eight people hiding in the Secret Annexe were arrested. Miep Gies and Bep Voskuijl, the two secretaries working in the building, found Anne's diaries strewn all over the floor. Miep Gies tucked them away in a desk drawer for safekeeping. After the war, when it became clear that Anne was dead, she gave the diaries, unread, to Anne's father, Otto Frank.

After long deliberation, Otto Frank decided to fulfil his daughter's wish and publish her diary. He selected material from versions *a* and *b*, editing them into a shorter version later referred to as version *c*. Readers all over the world know this as *The Diary of a Young Girl*.

In making his choice, Otto Frank had to bear several points in mind. To begin with, the book had to be kept short so that it would fit in with a series put out by the Dutch publisher. In addition, several passages dealing with Anne's sexuality were omitted; at the time of the diary's initial publication, in 1947, it was not customary to write openly about sex, and certainly not in books for young adults. Out of respect for the dead, Otto Frank also omitted a number of unflattering passages about his wife and the other residents of the Secret Annexe. Anne Frank, who was thirteen when she began her diary and fifteen when she was forced to stop, wrote without reserve about her likes and dislikes.

When Otto Frank died in 1980, he willed his daughter's manuscripts to the Netherlands State Institute for War Documentation in Amsterdam. Because the authenticity of the diary had been challenged ever since its publication, the Institute for War Documentation ordered a thorough investigation. Once the diary was proved, beyond a shadow of a doubt, to be genuine, it was published in its entirety, along with the results of an exhaustive study. *The Critical Edition* contains not only versions *a*, *b* and *c*, but also articles on the background of the Frank family, the circumstances surrounding their arrest and deportation, and the examination into Anne's handwriting, the document and the materials used.

The Anne Frank–Fonds (Anne Frank Foundation) in Basle (Switzerland), which as Otto Frank's sole heir had also inherited his daughter's copyrights, then decided to have a new, expanded edition of the diary published for general readers. This new edition in no way affects the integrity of the old one originally edited by Otto Frank, which brought the diary and its message to millions of people. The task of compiling the expanded edition was given to the writer and translator Mirjam Pressler. Otto Frank's original selection has now been supplemented with passages from Anne's *a* and *b* versions. Mirjam Pressler's definitive edition, approved by the Anne Frank–Fonds, contains approximately 30 per cent more material and is intended to give the reader more insight into the world of Anne Frank.

In writing her second version (*b*), Anne invented pseudonyms for the people who would appear in her book. She initially wanted to call herself Anne Aulis, and later Anne Robin. Otto Frank opted to call his family by their own names and to follow Anne's wishes with regard to the others. Over the years, the identity of the people who helped the families in the Secret Annexe has become common knowledge. In this edition, the helpers are now referred to by their real names, as they so justly deserve to be. All other persons are named in accordance with the pseudonyms in *The Critical Edition*. The Institute for War Documentation has arbitrarily assigned initials to those persons wishing to remain anonymous.

The real names of the other people hiding in the Secret Annexe are:

THE VAN PELS FAMILY

(from Osnabrück, Germany):

Auguste van Pels (born 9 September 1900)
Hermann van Pels (born 31 March 1898)
Peter van Pels (born 8 November 1926)

Called by Anne, in her manuscript: Petronella, Hans and Alfred van Daan; and in the book: Petronella, Hermann and Peter van Daan.

FRITZ PFEFFER

(born 30 April 1889, in Giessen, Germany):

Called by Anne, in her manuscript and in the book: Albert Dussel.

The reader may wish to bear in mind that much of this edition is based on the *b* version of Anne's diary, which she wrote when she was about fifteen years old. Occasionally, Anne went back and commented on a passage she had written earlier. These comments are clearly marked in this edition. Naturally, Anne's spelling and linguistic errors have been corrected. Otherwise, the text has basically been left as she wrote it, since any attempts at editing and clarification would be inappropriate in a historical document.

The Diary of a Young Girl

*Ik zal hoop ik aan jou alles kunnen
toevertrouwen, zoals ik het nog aan
niemand gekund heb, en ik hoop dat
je me een grote steun aan me zult zijn.*
Anne Frank. 12 Juni 1942.

I hope I will be able to confide everything
to you, as I have never been able to confide
in anyone, and I hope you will be a great
source of comfort and support.

I hope I will be able to confide everything to you, as I have never been able to confide in anyone, and I hope you will be a great source of comfort and support.

COMMENT ADDED BY ANNE ON 28 SEPTEMBER 1942: *So far you truly have been a great source of comfort to me, and so has Kitty, whom I now write to regularly. This way of keeping a diary is much nicer, and now I can hardly wait for those moments when I'm able to write in you.*

Oh, I'm so glad I brought you along!

SUNDAY, 14 JUNE 1942

I'll begin from the moment I got you, the moment I saw you lying on the table among my other birthday presents. (I went along when you were bought, but that doesn't count.)

On Friday, 12 June, I was awake at six o'clock, which isn't surprising, since it was my birthday. But I'm not allowed to get up at that hour, so I had to control my curiosity until quarter to seven. When I couldn't wait any longer, I went to the dining-room, where Moortje (the cat) welcomed me by rubbing against my legs.

A little after seven I went to Daddy and Mummy and then to the living-room to open my presents, and *you* were the first thing I saw, maybe one of my nicest presents. Then a bouquet of roses, some peonies and a potted plant. From Daddy and Mummy I got a blue blouse, a game, a bottle of grape juice, which to my mind tastes a bit like wine (after all, wine is made from grapes), a puzzle, a jar of cold cream, 2.50 guilders and a gift token for two books. I got another book as well, *Camera Obscura* (but Margot already has it, so I exchanged mine for something else), a plate of homemade biscuits (which I made myself, of course, since I've become quite an expert at making biscuits), lots of sweets and a strawberry tart from Mother. And a letter from Grammy, right on time, but of course that was just a coincidence.

Then Hanneli came to pick me up, and we went to school. During break I handed out biscuits to my teachers and my class, and then it was time to get back to work. I didn't arrive home until five, since I went to gym with the rest of the class. (I'm not allowed to take part because my shoulders and hips tend to get dislocated.) As it was my birthday, I could decide which game my classmates would play, and I chose volleyball. Afterwards they all danced around me in a circle and sang 'Happy Birthday'. When I got home, Sanne Ledermann was already there. Ilse Wagner, Hanneli Goslar and Jacqueline van Maarsen came home with me after gym, since we're in the same class. Hanneli and Sanne used to be my two best friends. People who saw us together used to say, 'There goes Anne, Hanne and Sanne.' I only met Jacqueline van Maarsen when I started at the Jewish Lyceum, and now she's my best friend. Ilse is Hanneli's best friend, and Sanne goes to another school and has friends there.

They gave me a beautiful book, *Dutch Sagas and Legends*,

but they gave me Volume II by mistake, so I exchanged two other books for Volume I. Aunt Helene brought me a puzzle, Aunt Stephanie a darling brooch and Aunt Leny a terrific book: *Daisy Goes to the Mountains*.

This morning I lay in the bath thinking how wonderful it would be if I had a dog like Rin Tin Tin. I'd call him Rin Tin Tin too, and I'd take him to school with me, where he could stay in the caretaker's room or by the bicycle racks when the weather was good.

I had my birthday party on Sunday afternoon. The Rin Tin Tin film was a big hit with my classmates. I got two brooches, a bookmark and two books.

I'll start by saying a few things about my school and my class, beginning with the other children.

Betty Bloemendaal looks rather poor, and I think she probably is. She lives on an obscure street in West Amsterdam, and none of us knows where it is. She does very well at school, but that's because she works so hard, not because she's clever. She's pretty quiet.

Jacqueline van Maarsen is supposedly my best friend, but I've never had a real friend. At first I thought Jacque would be one, but I was badly mistaken.

D.Q.* is a very nervous girl who's always forgetting things, so the teachers keep giving her extra homework as a punishment. She's very kind, especially to G.Z.

E.S. talks so much it isn't funny. She's always touching

---

* Initials have been assigned at random to those persons who prefer to remain anonymous.

3

your hair or fiddling with your buttons when she asks you something. They say she can't stand me, but I don't care, because I don't like her much either.

Henny Mets is a nice girl with a cheerful disposition, except that she talks in a loud voice and is really childish when we're playing outside. Unfortunately, Henny has a girlfriend named Beppy who's a bad influence on her because she's dirty and vulgar.

J.R. – I could write a whole book about her. J. is a detestable, sneaky, stuck-up, two-faced gossip who thinks she's so grown-up. She's really got Jacque under her spell, and that's a shame. J. is easily offended, bursts into tears at the slightest thing and, to top it all, is a terrible show-off. Miss J. always has to be right. She's very rich, and has a wardrobe full of the most adorable dresses that are much too old for her. She thinks she's gorgeous, but she's not. J. and I can't stand each other.

Ilse Wagner is a nice girl with a cheerful disposition, but she's extremely finicky and can spend hours moaning and groaning about something. Ilse likes me a lot. She's very clever, but lazy.

Hanneli Goslar, or Lies as she's called at school, is a bit on the strange side. She's usually shy – outspoken at home, but reserved with other people. She blabs whatever you tell her to her mother. But she says what she thinks, and lately I've come to appreciate her a great deal.

Nannie van Praag-Sigaar is small, funny and sensible. I think she's nice. She's pretty clever. There isn't much else you can say about Nannie.

Eefje de Jong is, in my opinion, terrific. Though she's only twelve, she's quite the lady. She treats me like a baby. She's also very helpful, and I like her.

G.Z. is the prettiest girl in our class. She has a nice face, but is a bit stupid. I think they're going to hold her back a year, but of course I haven't told her that.

COMMENT ADDED BY ANNE AT A LATER DATE:
To my great surprise, G.Z. wasn't held back a year after all.

And sitting next to G.Z. is the last of us twelve girls, me.

There's a lot to be said about the boys, or maybe not so much after all.

Maurice Coster is one of my many admirers, but pretty much of a pest.

Sallie Springer has a filthy mind, and rumour has it that he's gone all the way. Still, I think he's terrific, because he's very funny.

Emiel Bonewit is G.Z.'s admirer, but she doesn't care. He's pretty boring.

Rob Cohen used to be in love with me too, but I can't stand him any more. He's an obnoxious, two-faced, lying, snivelling little twit with an awfully high opinion of himself.

Max van de Velde is a farm boy from Medemblik, but a decent sort, as Margot would say.

Herman Koopman also has a filthy mind, just like Jopie de Beer, who's a terrible flirt and girl-chaser.

Leo Blom is Jopie de Beer's best friend, but has been spoiled by Jopie's dirty mind.

Albert de Mesquita came from the Montessori School and jumped a year. He's really clever.

Leo Slager came from the same school, but isn't as clever.

Ru Stoppelmon is a short, goofy boy from Almelo who transferred to this school in the middle of the year.

C.N. does whatever he's not supposed to.

Jacques Kocernoot sits behind us, next to C., and we (G. and I) laugh ourselves stupid.

Harry Schaap is the most decent boy in our class. He's nice.

Werner Joseph is nice too, but all the changes taking place lately have made him too quiet, so he seems boring.

Sam Salomon is one of those tough guys from the rough part of town. A real brat. (Admirer!)

Appie Riem is pretty Orthodox, but a brat too.

Writing in a diary is a really strange experience for someone like me. Not only because I've never written anything before, but also because it seems to me that later on neither I nor anyone else will be interested in the musings of a thirteen-year-old schoolgirl. Oh well, it doesn't matter. I feel like writing, and I have an even greater need to get all kinds of things off my chest.

'Paper has more patience than people.' I thought of this saying on one of those days when I was feeling a little depressed and was sitting at home with my chin in my hands, bored and listless, wondering whether to stay in or go out. I finally stayed where I was, brooding. Yes, paper *does* have more patience, and since I'm not planning to let anyone else read this stiff-backed notebook grandly referred to as a 'diary', unless I should ever find a real friend, it probably won't make a bit of difference.

Now I'm back to the point that prompted me to keep a diary in the first place: I don't have a friend.

Let me put it more clearly, since no one will believe that a thirteen-year-old girl is completely alone in the world. And I'm not. I have loving parents and a sixteen-year-old sister, and there are about thirty people I can call friends. I have a throng of admirers who can't keep their adoring eyes off me and who sometimes have to resort to using a broken pocket mirror to try and catch a glimpse of me in the classroom. I have a family, loving aunts and a good home. No, on the surface I seem to have everything, except my one true friend. All I think about when I'm with friends is having a good time. I can't bring myself to talk about anything but ordinary everyday things. We don't seem to be able to get any closer, and that's the problem. Maybe it's my fault that we don't confide in each other. In any case, that's just how things are, and unfortunately they're not liable to change. This is why I've started the diary.

To enhance the image of this long-awaited friend in my imagination, I don't want to jot down the facts in this diary the way most people would do, but I want the diary to be my friend, and I'm going to call this friend *Kitty*.

Since no one would understand a word of my stories to Kitty if I were to plunge right in, I'd better provide a brief sketch of my life, much as I dislike doing so.

My father, the most adorable father I've ever seen, didn't marry my mother until he was thirty-six and she was twenty-five. My sister Margot was born in Frankfurt am Main in Germany in 1926. I was born on 12 June 1929. I lived in Frankfurt until I was four. Because we're Jewish, my father emigrated to Holland in 1933, when he became the Managing Director of the Dutch Opekta Company, which manufactures products used in making jam. My mother, Edith Holländer Frank, went with him to Holland in September, while Margot and I were sent to Aachen to stay with our grandmother. Margot went to Holland in December, and I followed in February, when I was plonked down on the table as a birthday present for Margot.

I started right away at the Montessori nursery school. I stayed there until I was six, at which time I started in the first form. In the sixth form my teacher was Mrs Kuperus, the headmistress. At the end of the year we were both in tears as we said a heartbreaking farewell, because I'd been accepted at the Jewish Lyceum, where Margot also went to school.

Our lives were not without anxiety, since our relatives in Germany were suffering under Hitler's anti-Jewish laws. After the pogroms in 1938 my two uncles (my mother's brothers) fled Germany, finding safe refuge in North America. My elderly grandmother came to live with us. She was seventy-three years old at the time.

After May 1940 the good times were few and far between: first there was the war, then the capitulation and then the arrival of the Germans, which is when the trouble started for the Jews. Our freedom was severely restricted by a series of anti-Jewish decrees: Jews were required to wear a yellow star; Jews were required to turn in their bicycles; Jews were forbidden to use trams; Jews were forbidden to ride in cars, even their own; Jews were required to do their shopping between 3.00 and 5.00 p.m.; Jews were required to frequent only Jewish-owned barbershops and beauty salons; Jews were forbidden to be out on the streets between 8.00 p.m. and 6.00 a.m.; Jews were forbidden to go to theatres, cinemas or any other forms of entertainment; Jews were forbidden to use swimming pools, tennis courts, hockey fields or any other athletic fields; Jews were forbidden to go rowing; Jews were forbidden to take part in any athletic activity in public; Jews were forbidden to sit in their gardens or those of their friends after 8.00 p.m.; Jews were forbidden to visit Christians in their homes; Jews were required to attend Jewish schools, etc. You couldn't do this and you couldn't do that, but life went on. Jacque always said to me, 'I don't dare do anything any more, 'cause I'm afraid it's not allowed.'

In the summer of 1941 Grandma fell ill and had to have an operation, so my birthday passed with little celebration. In the summer of 1940 we didn't do much for my birthday either, since the fighting had just ended in Holland. Grandma died in January 1942. No one knows how often I think of her and still love her. This birthday celebration in 1942 was intended to make up for the others, and Grandma's candle was lit along with the rest.

The four of us are still doing well, and that brings me to the present date of 20 June 1942, and the solemn dedication of my diary.

SATURDAY, 20 JUNE 1942

Dearest Kitty!

Let me get started right away; it's nice and quiet now. Father and Mother are out and Margot has gone to play ping-pong with some other young people at her friend Trees's. I've been playing a lot of ping-pong myself lately. So much that five of us girls have formed a club. It's called 'The Little Dipper Minus Two'. A really silly name, but it's based on a mistake. We wanted to give our club a special name; and because there were five of us, we came up with the idea of the Little Dipper. We thought it consisted of five stars, but we turned out to be wrong. It has seven, like the Big Dipper, which explains the 'Minus Two'. Ilse Wagner has a ping-pong set, and the Wagners let us play in their big dining-room whenever we want. Since we five ping-pong players like ice-cream, especially in the summer, and since you get hot playing ping-pong, our games usually end with a visit to the nearest ice-cream parlour that allows Jews: either Oasis or Delphi. We've long since stopped hunting around for our purses or money – most of the time it's so busy in Oasis that we manage to find a few generous young men of our acquaintance or an admirer to offer us more ice-cream than we could eat in a week.

You're probably a little surprised to hear me talking about admirers at such a tender age. Unfortunately, or not, as the case may be, this vice seems to be rampant at our school. As soon as a boy asks if he can cycle home with me and we start talking, nine times out of ten I can be sure he'll become enamoured on the spot and won't let me out of his sight for a second. His ardour eventually cools, especially since I ignore his passionate glances and pedal blithely on my way. If it gets so bad that they start rambling on about 'asking Father's permission', I swerve slightly on my bike, my satchel falls, and the young man feels obliged to get off his bike and hand it to me, by which time I've switched the conversation to another topic. These are the most innocent types. Of course, there are those who blow you kisses or try to take hold of your arm, but they're definitely knocking on the wrong door. I get off my bike and either refuse to make further use of their company or act as if I'm insulted and tell them in no uncertain terms to go on home without me.

There you are. We've now laid the basis for our friendship. Until tomorrow.

Yours, Anne

SUNDAY, 21 JUNE 1942

Dearest Kitty,

Our entire class is quaking in its boots. The reason, of course, is the forthcoming meeting in which the teachers decide who'll move up to the next form and who'll be kept back. Half the class is making bets. G.Z. and I laugh ourselves silly at the two boys behind us, C.N. and Jacques Kocernoot, who have staked their entire holiday savings on their bet. From morning to night, it's 'You're going to pass', 'No, I'm not', 'Yes, you are', 'No, I'm not'. Even G.'s pleading glances and my angry outbursts can't calm them down. If you ask me, there are so many dummies that about a quarter of the class should be kept back, but teachers are the most unpredictable creatures on earth. Maybe this time they'll be unpredictable in the right direction for a change.

I'm not so worried about my girlfriends and myself. We'll make it. The only subject I'm not sure about is maths. Anyway, all we can do is wait. Until then, we keep telling each other not to lose heart.

I get along pretty well with all my teachers. There are nine of them, seven men and two women. Mr Keesing, the old fogey who teaches maths, was annoyed with me for ages because I talked so much. After several warnings, he assigned me extra homework. An essay on the subject 'A Chatterbox'. A chatterbox, what can you write about that? I'd worry about that later, I decided. I jotted down the title in my notebook, tucked it in my bag and tried to keep quiet.

That evening, after I'd finished the rest of my homework, the note about the essay caught my eye. I began thinking about the subject while chewing the tip of my fountain pen. Anyone could ramble on and leave big spaces between the words, but the trick was to come up with convincing arguments to prove the necessity of talking. I thought and thought, and suddenly I had an idea. I wrote the three pages Mr Keesing had assigned me and was satisfied. I argued that talking is a female trait and that I would do my best to keep it under control, but that I would never be able to cure myself of the habit, since my mother talked as much as I did, if not more, and that there's not much you can do about inherited traits.

Mr Keesing had a good laugh at my arguments, but when I proceeded to talk my way through the next lesson, he assigned me a second essay. This time it was supposed to be on 'An Incorrigible Chatterbox'. I handed it in, and Mr Keesing had nothing to complain about for two whole lessons. However, during the third lesson he'd finally had enough. 'Anne Frank, as punishment for talking in class, write an essay entitled "'Quack, Quack, Quack,' Said Mistress Chatterback".'

The class roared. I had to laugh too, though I'd nearly exhausted my ingenuity on the topic of chatterboxes. It was time to come up with something else, something original. My friend Sanne, who's good at poetry, offered to help me write the essay from beginning to end in verse. I jumped for joy. Keesing was trying to play a joke on me with this ridiculous subject, but I'd make sure the joke was on him.

I finished my poem, and it was beautiful! It was about a mother duck and a father swan with three baby ducklings who were bitten to death by the father because they quacked too much. Luckily, Keesing took the joke the right way. He read the poem to the class, adding his own comments, and to several other classes as well. Since then I've been allowed to talk and haven't been assigned any extra homework. On the contrary, Keesing's always making jokes these days.

Yours, Anne

WEDNESDAY, 24 JUNE 1942

Dearest Kitty,

It's sweltering. Everyone is huffing and puffing, and in this heat I have to walk everywhere. Only now do I realize how pleasant a tram is, but we Jews are no longer allowed to make use of this luxury; our own two feet are good enough for us. Yesterday at lunchtime I had an appointment with the dentist on Jan Luykenstraat. It's a long way from our school on Stadstimmertuinen. That afternoon I nearly fell asleep at my desk. Fortunately, people automatically offer you something to drink. The dental nurse is really kind.

The only mode of transport left to us is the ferry. The ferryman at Josef Israëlkade took us across when we asked him to. It's not the fault of the Dutch that we Jews are having such a bad time.

I wish I didn't have to go to school. My bike was stolen during the Easter holidays, and Father gave Mother's bike to some Christian friends for safekeeping. Thank goodness the summer holidays are almost here; one more week and our torment will be over.

Something unexpected happened yesterday morning. As I was passing the bicycle racks, I heard my name being called. I turned around and there was the nice boy I'd met the evening before at my friend Wilma's. He's Wilma's second cousin. I used to think Wilma was nice, which she is, but all she ever talks about is boys, and that gets to be a bore. He came towards me, somewhat shyly, and introduced himself as Hello Silberberg. I was a little surprised and wasn't sure what he wanted, but it didn't take me long to find out. He asked if I would allow him to accompany me to school. 'As long as you're headed that way, I'll go with you,' I said. And so we walked together. Hello is sixteen and good at telling all kinds of funny stories.

He was waiting for me again this morning, and I expect he will be from now on.

Anne

Dearest Kitty,

Until today I honestly couldn't find the time to write to you. I was with friends all day Thursday, we had company on Friday, and that's how it went until today.

Hello and I have got to know each other very well this past week, and he's told me a lot about his life. He comes from Gelsenkirchen and is living with his grandparents. His parents are in Belgium, but there's no way he can get there. Hello used to have a girlfriend named Ursula. I know her too. She's perfectly sweet and perfectly boring. Ever since he met me, Hello has realized that he's been falling asleep at Ursul's side. So I'm kind of a pep tonic. You never know what you're good for!

Jacque spent Saturday night here. Sunday afternoon she was at Hanneli's, and I was bored stiff.

Hello was supposed to come over that evening, but he rang about six. I answered the phone, and he said, 'This is Helmuth Silberberg. May I please speak to Anne?'

'Oh, Hello. This is Anne.'

'Oh, hello, Anne. How are you?'

'Very well, thanks.'

'I just wanted to say I'm sorry but I can't come tonight, though I would like to have a word with you. Is it all right if I come by and pick up you in about ten minutes?'

'Yes, that's fine. Bye-bye!'

'Okay, I'll be right over. Bye-bye!'

I hung up, quickly changed my clothes and did my hair. I was so nervous I leaned out of the window to watch for him. He finally showed up. Miracle of miracles, I didn't rush down the stairs, but waited quietly until he rang the bell. I went down to open the door, and he got right to the point.

'Anne, my grandmother thinks you're too young for me to be seeing you on a regular basis. She says I should be going to the Lowenbachs', but you probably know that I'm not going out with Ursul any more.'

'No, I didn't know. What happened? Did you two have an argument?'

'No, nothing like that. I told Ursul that we weren't suited to each other and so it was better for us not to go out together any more, but that she was welcome at my house and I hoped I would be welcome at hers. Actually, I thought Ursul was hanging around with another boy, and I treated her as if she were. But that wasn't true. And then my uncle said I should apologize to her, but of course I didn't feel like it, and that's why I broke up with her. But that was just one of the reasons.

'Now my grandmother wants me to see Ursul and not you, but I don't agree and I'm not going to. Sometimes old people have really old-fashioned ideas, but that doesn't mean I have to go along with them. I need my grandparents, but in a certain sense they need me too. From now on I'll be free on Wednesday evenings. You see, my grandparents made me sign up for a wood-carving class, but actually I go to a club organized by the Zionists. My grandparents don't want me to go, because they're anti-Zionists. I'm not a fanatical Zionist, but it interests me. Anyway, it's been such a mess lately that I'm planning to leave. So next Wednesday will be my last meeting. That means I can see you Wednesday evening, Saturday afternoon, Saturday evening, Sunday afternoon and maybe even more.'

'But if your grandparents don't want you to, you shouldn't go behind their backs.'

'All's fair in love and war.'

Just then we passed Blankevoort's Bookshop and there

was Peter Schiff with two other boys; it was the first time he'd said hello to me in ages, and it really made me feel good.

Monday evening Hello came over to meet Father and Mother. I had bought a cake and some sweets, and we had tea and biscuits, the works, but neither Hello nor I felt like sitting stiffly on our chairs. So we went out for a walk, and he didn't deliver me to my door until ten past eight. Father was furious. He said it was very wrong of me not to get home on time. I had to promise to be home by ten to eight in future. I've been asked to Hello's on Saturday.

Wilma told me that one night when Hello was at her house, she asked him, 'Who do you like best, Ursul or Anne?'

He said, 'It's none of your business.'

But as he was leaving (they hadn't talked to each other the rest of the evening), he said, 'Well, I like Anne better, but don't tell anyone. Bye!' And whoosh . . . he was out of the door.

In everything he says or does, I can see that Hello is in love with me, and it's kind of nice for a change. Margot would say that Hello is a decent sort. I think so too, but he's more than that. Mother is also full of praise: 'A good-looking boy. Nice and polite.' I'm glad he's so popular with everyone. Except with my girlfriends. He thinks they're very childish, and he's right about that. Jacque still teases me about him, but I'm not in love with him. Not really. It's all right for me to have boys as friends. Nobody minds.

Mother is always asking me who I'm going to marry when I grow up, but I bet she'll never guess it's Peter, because I talked her out of that idea myself, without batting an eyelash. I love Peter as I've never loved anyone, and I tell myself he's only going around with all those other girls to hide his feelings for me. Maybe he thinks Hello and I are in love with each other, which we're not. He's just a friend, or as Mother puts it, a suitor.

Yours, Anne

SUNDAY, 5 JULY 1942

Dear Kitty,

The examination results were announced in the Jewish Theatre on Friday. My report wasn't too bad. I got one D, a C− in algebra and all the rest Bs, except for two B+s and two B−s. My parents are pleased, but they're not like other parents when it comes to grades. They never worry about reports, good or bad. As long as I'm healthy and happy and not too cheeky, they're satisfied. If these three things are all right, everything else will take care of itself.

I'm just the opposite. I don't want to be a bad pupil. I was accepted at the Jewish Lyceum on a conditional basis. I was supposed to stay at the Montessori School, but when Jewish children were required to go to Jewish schools, Mr Elte finally agreed, after a great deal of persuasion, to accept Lies Goslar and me. Lies also passed this year, though she has to repeat her geometry exam.

Poor Lies. It isn't easy for her to study at home; her baby sister, a spoiled little two-year-old, plays in her room all day. If Gabi doesn't get her way, she starts screaming, and if Lies doesn't look after her, Mrs Goslar starts screaming. So Lies has a hard time doing her homework, and as long as that's the case, the extra tuition she's been getting won't help much. The Goslar household is really a sight. Mrs Goslar's parents live next door, but eat with the family. Then there's the hired help, the baby, the always absent-minded and absent Mr Goslar and the always nervous and

17

irritable Mrs Goslar, who's expecting another baby. Lies, who's all thumbs, gets lost in the mayhem.

My sister Margot has also got her report. Brilliant, as usual. If we had such a thing as 'cum laude', she would have passed with honours, she's so clever.

Father has been home a lot lately. There's nothing for him to do at the office; it must be awful to feel you're not needed. Mr Kleiman has taken over Opekta, and Mr Kugler, Gies & Co., the company dealing in spices and spice substitutes that was set up in 1941.

A few days ago, as we were taking a stroll around our neighbourhood square, Father began to talk about going into hiding. He said it would be very hard for us to live cut off from the rest of the world. I asked him why he was bringing this up now.

'Well, Anne,' he replied, 'you know that for more than a year we've been sending our clothes, food and furniture to other people. We don't want our belongings to be seized by the Germans. Nor do we want to fall into their clutches ourselves. So we'll leave of our own accord and not wait to be hauled away.'

'But when, Father?' He sounded so serious that I felt scared.

'Don't you worry. We'll take care of everything. Just enjoy your carefree life while you can.'

That was it. Oh, may these sombre words not come true for as long as possible.

The doorbell's ringing, Hello's here, time to stop.

Yours, Anne

Dearest Kitty,

It seems like years since Sunday morning. So much has happened it's as if the whole world had suddenly turned upside down. But as you can see, Kitty, I'm still alive, and that's the main thing, Father says. I'm alive all right, but don't ask where or how. You probably don't understand a word I'm saying today, so I'll begin by telling you what happened Sunday afternoon.

At three o'clock (Hello had left but was supposed to come back later), the doorbell rang. I didn't hear it, since I was out on the balcony, lazily reading in the sun. A little while later Margot appeared in the kitchen doorway looking very agitated. 'Father has received a call-up notice from the SS,' she whispered. 'Mother has gone to see Mr van Daan.' (Mr van Daan is Father's business partner and a good friend.)

I was stunned. A call-up: everyone knows what that means. Visions of concentration camps and lonely cells raced through my head. How could we let Father go to such a fate? 'Of course he's not going,' declared Margot as we waited for Mother in the living-room. 'Mother's gone to Mr van Daan to ask whether we can move to our hiding place tomorrow. The van Daans are going with us. There will be seven of us altogether.' Silence. We couldn't speak. The thought of Father off visiting someone in the Jewish Hospital and completely unaware of what was happening, the long wait for Mother, the heat, the suspense – all this reduced us to silence.

Suddenly the doorbell rang again. 'That's Hello,' I said.

'Don't open the door!' exclaimed Margot to stop me. But it wasn't necessary, since we heard Mother and Mr van Daan downstairs talking to Hello, and then the two of them came inside and shut the door behind them. Every time the bell rang, either Margot or I had to tiptoe downstairs to see if it was Father, and we didn't let anyone else in. Margot and I were sent from the room, as Mr van Daan wanted to talk to Mother alone.

When she and I were sitting in our bedroom, Margot told me that the call-up was not for Father, but for her. At this second shock, I began to cry. Margot is sixteen – apparently they want to send girls her age away on their own. But thank goodness she won't be going; Mother had said so herself, which must be what Father had meant when he talked to me about our going into hiding. Hiding . . . where would we hide? In the city? In the country? In a house? In a shack? When, where, how . . . ? These were questions I wasn't allowed to ask, but they still kept running through my mind.

Margot and I started packing our most important belongings into a satchel. The first thing I stuck in was this diary, and then curlers, handkerchiefs, schoolbooks, a comb and some old letters. Preoccupied by the thought of going into hiding, I stuck the craziest things in the satchel, but I'm not sorry. Memories mean more to me than dresses.

Father finally came home around five o'clock, and we rang Mr Kleiman to ask if he could come by that evening. Mr van Daan left and went to get Miep. Miep arrived and promised to return later that night, taking with her a bag full of shoes, dresses, jackets, underwear and stockings. After that it was quiet in our flat; none of us felt like eating. It was still hot, and everything was very strange.

We had rented out our big upstairs room to a Mr Gold-schmidt, a divorced man in his thirties, who apparently had nothing to do that evening, since despite all our polite hints he hung around until ten o'clock.

Miep and Jan Gies came at eleven. Miep, who's worked

for Father's company since 1933, has become a close friend, and so has her husband Jan. Once again, shoes, stockings, books and underwear disappeared into Miep's bag and Jan's deep pockets. At eleven-thirty they too disappeared.

I was exhausted, and even though I knew it'd be my last night in my own bed, I fell asleep right away and didn't wake up until Mother called me at five-thirty the next morning. Fortunately, it wasn't as hot as Sunday; a warm rain fell throughout the day. The four of us were wrapped in so many layers of clothes it looked as if we were going off to spend the night in a refrigerator, and all that just so we could take more clothes with us. No Jew in our situation would dare leave the house with a suitcase full of clothes. I was wearing two vests, three pairs of pants, a dress, and over that a skirt, a jacket, a raincoat, two pairs of stockings, heavy shoes, a cap, a scarf and lots more. I was suffocating even before we left the house, but no one bothered to ask me how I felt.

Margot stuffed her satchel with schoolbooks, went to get her bicycle and, with Miep leading the way, rode off into the great unknown. At any rate, that's how I thought of it, since I still didn't know where our hiding place was.

At seven-thirty we too closed the door behind us; Moortje, my cat, was the only living creature I said good-bye to. According to a note we left for Mr Goldschmidt, she was to be taken to the neighbours, who would give her a good home.

The stripped beds, the breakfast things on the table, the pound of meat for the cat in the kitchen – all of these created the impression that we'd left in a hurry. But we weren't interested in impressions. We just wanted to get out of there, to get away and reach our destination in safety. Nothing else mattered.

More tomorrow.

Yours, Anne

Dearest Kitty,

So there we were, Father, Mother and I, walking in the pouring rain, each of us with a satchel and a shopping bag filled to the brim with the most varied assortment of items. The people on their way to work at that early hour gave us sympathetic looks; you could tell by their faces that they were sorry they couldn't offer us some kind of transport; the conspicuous yellow star spoke for itself.

Only when we were walking down the street did Father and Mother reveal, little by little, what the plan was. For months we'd been moving as much of our furniture and apparel out of the flat as we could. It was agreed that we'd go into hiding on 16 July. Because of Margot's call-up notice, the plan had to be moved forward ten days, which meant we'd have to make do with less orderly rooms.

The hiding place was located in Father's office building. That's a little hard for outsiders to understand, so I'll explain. Father didn't have a lot of people working in his office, just Mr Kugler, Mr Kleiman, Miep and a twenty-three-year-old typist named Bep Voskuijl, all of whom were informed of our coming. Mr Voskuijl, Bep's father, works in the warehouse, along with two assistants, none of whom were told anything.

Here's a description of the building. The large warehouse on the ground floor is used as a workroom and storeroom and is divided into several different sections, such as the stockroom and the milling room, where cinnamon, cloves and a pepper substitute are ground.

Next to the warehouse doors is another outside door, a separate entrance to the office. Just inside the office door is a second door, and beyond that a stairway. At the top of the stairs is another door, with a frosted window on which the word 'Office' is written in black letters. This is the big front office – very large, very light and very full. Bep, Miep and Mr Kleiman work there during the day. After passing through an alcove containing a safe, a wardrobe and a big stationery cupboard, you come to the small, dark, stuffy back office. This used to be shared by Mr Kugler and Mr van Daan, but now Mr Kugler is its only occupant. Mr Kugler's office can also be reached from the passage, but only through a glass door that can be opened from the inside but not easily from the outside. If you leave Mr Kugler's office and proceed through the long, narrow passage past the coal store and go up four steps, you find yourself in the private office, the showpiece of the entire building. Elegant mahogany furniture, a linoleum floor covered with rugs, a radio, a fancy lamp, everything first class. Next door is a spacious kitchen with a water-heater and two gas rings, and beside that a lavatory. That's the first floor.

A wooden staircase leads from the downstairs passage to the second floor. At the top of the stairs is a landing, with doors on either side. The door on the left takes you up to the spice storage area, attic and loft in the front part of the house. A typically Dutch, very steep, ankle-twisting flight of stairs also runs from the front part of the house to another door opening on to the street.

The door to the right of the landing leads to the 'Secret Annexe' at the back of the house. No one would ever suspect there were so many rooms behind that plain grey door. There's just one small step in front of the door, and then you're inside. Straight ahead of you is a steep flight of stairs. To the left is a narrow hallway opening on to a room that serves as the Frank family's living-room and bedroom. Next door is a smaller room, the bedroom and study of the two

1st Floor

Private Office · Kitchen · Back Office · Alcove · Front Office · Bookcase

2nd Floor

Bed · Bed · Bed · Bed · Storeroom · Storeroom · Storeroom · Landing

3rd Floor

Folding Bed · Table · Bed · Kitchen Surface · Bed · Flat Roof · Front Attic

1st Floor   2nd Floor   3rd Floor

young ladies of the family. To the right of the stairs is a 'bathroom', a windowless room with just a sink. The door in the corner leads to the lavatory and another one to Margot's and my room. If you go up the stairs and open the door at the top, you're surprised to see such a large, light and spacious room in an old canalside house like this. It contains a gas cooker (thanks to the fact that it used to be Mr Kugler's laboratory) and a sink. This will be the kitchen and bedroom of Mr and Mrs van Daan, as well as the general living-room, dining-room and study for us all. A tiny side room is to be Peter van Daan's bedroom. Then, just as in the front part of the building, there's an attic and a loft. So there you are. Now I've introduced you to the whole of our lovely Annexe!

Yours, Anne

Dearest Kitty,

I've probably bored you with my long description of our house, but I still think you should know where I've ended up; how I ended up here is something you'll work out from my next letters.

But first, let me continue my story, because, as you know, I hadn't finished. After we arrived at 263 Prinsengracht, Miep quickly led us through the long passage and up the wooden staircase to the next floor and into the Annexe. She shut the door behind us, leaving us alone. Margot had arrived much earlier on her bike and was waiting for us.

Our living-room and all the other rooms were so full of stuff that I can't find the words to describe it. All the cardboard boxes that had been sent to the office in the last few months were piled on the floors and beds. The small room was filled from floor to ceiling with linen. If we wanted to sleep in properly made beds that night, we had to get going and tidy up the mess. Mother and Margot were unable to move a muscle. They lay down on their bare mattresses, tired, miserable and I don't know what else. But Father and I, the two cleaner-uppers in the family, started in right away.

All day long we unpacked boxes, filled cupboards, hammered nails and tidied up the mess, until we fell exhausted into our clean beds at night. We hadn't eaten a hot meal all day, but we didn't care; Mother and Margot were too tired and keyed up to eat, and Father and I were too busy.

Tuesday morning we started where we left off the night before. Bep and Miep went shopping with our ration coupons, Father worked on our black-out screens, we scrubbed the kitchen floor, and were once again busy from morning to night. Until Wednesday, I didn't have a chance to think about the enormous change in my life. Then for the first time since our arrival in the Secret Annexe, I found a moment to tell you all about it and to realize what had happened to me and what was yet to happen.

Yours, Anne

SATURDAY, 11 JULY 1942

Dearest Kitty,

Father, Mother and Margot still can't get used to the chiming of the Westertoren clock, which tells us the time every quarter of an hour. Not me, I liked it from the start; it sounds so reassuring, especially at night. You no doubt want to hear what I think of being in hiding. Well, all I can say is that I don't really know yet. I don't think I'll ever feel at home in this house, but that doesn't mean I hate it. It's more like being on holiday in some strange pension. Kind of an odd way to look at life in hiding, but that's how things are. The Annexe is an ideal place to hide in. It may be damp and lopsided, but there's probably not a more comfortable hiding place in all of Amsterdam. No, in all of Holland.

Up till now our bedroom, with its blank walls, was very bare. Thanks to Father – who brought my entire postcard and film-star collection here beforehand – and to a brush and a pot of glue, I was able to plaster the walls with pictures. It looks much more cheerful. When the van Daans arrive, we'll be able to build cupboards and other odds and ends out of the wood piled in the attic.

Margot and Mother have recovered somewhat. Yesterday Mother felt well enough to cook split-pea soup for the first time, but then she was downstairs talking and forgot all about it. The beans were scorched black, and no amount of scraping could get them out of the pan.

Last night the four of us went down to the private office and listened to England on the wireless. I was so scared someone might hear it that I literally begged Father to take me back upstairs. Mother understood my anxiety and went with me. Whatever we do, we're very afraid the neighbours might hear or see us. We started off immediately the first day sewing curtains. Actually, you can hardly call them that, since they're nothing but scraps of fabric, varying greatly in shape, quality and pattern, which Father and I stitched crookedly together with unskilled fingers. These works of art were tacked to the windows, where they'll stay until we come out of hiding.

The building on our right is a branch of the Keg Company, a firm from Zaandam, and on the left is a furniture workshop. Though the people who work there are not on the premises after hours, any sound we make might travel through the walls. We've forbidden Margot to cough at night, even though she has a bad cold, and are giving her large doses of codeine.

I'm looking forward to the arrival of the van Daans, which is set for Tuesday. It will be much more fun and also not as quiet. You see, it's the silence that makes me so nervous during the evenings and nights, and I'd give anything to have one of our helpers sleep here.

It's really not that bad here, since we can do our own cooking and can listen to the wireless in Daddy's office. Mr

Kleiman and Miep, and Bep Voskuijl too, have helped us so much. We've already preserved loads of rhubarb, strawberries and cherries, so for the time being I doubt we'll be bored. We also have a supply of reading material, and we're going to buy lots of games. Of course, we can't ever look out of the window or go outside. And we have to be quiet so the people downstairs can't hear us.

Yesterday we had our hands full. We had to pit two crates of cherries for Mr Kugler to preserve. We're going to use the empty crates to make bookshelves.

Someone's calling me.

Yours, Anne

COMMENT ADDED BY ANNE ON 28 SEPTEMBER 1942: *Not being able to go outside upsets me more than I can say, and I'm terrified our hiding place will be discovered and that we'll be shot. That, of course, is a fairly dismal prospect.*

SUNDAY, 12 JULY 1942

They were all so nice to me a month ago because of my birthday, and yet every day I feel myself drifting further away from Mother and Margot. I worked hard today and they praised me, only to start picking on me again five minutes later.

You can easily see the difference between the way they deal with Margot and the way they deal with me. For example, Margot broke the vacuum cleaner, and because of that we've been without light for the rest of the day. Mother said, 'Well, Margot, it's easy to see you're not used to working; otherwise, you'd have known better than to yank the plug out by the cord.' Margot made some reply, and that was the end of the story.

But this afternoon, when I wanted to rewrite something on Mother's shopping list because her handwriting is so hard to read, she wouldn't let me. She ticked me off again, and the whole family got involved.

I don't fit in with them, and I've felt that clearly in the last few weeks. They're so sentimental together, but I'd rather be sentimental on my own. They're always saying how nice it is with the four of us, and that we get along so well, without giving a moment's thought to the fact that I don't feel that way.

Daddy's the only one who understands me, now and again, though he usually sides with Mother and Margot. Another thing I can't stand is having them talk about me in front of outsiders, telling them how I cried or how sensibly I'm behaving. It's horrible. And sometimes they talk about Moortje and I can't bear that. Moortje is my weak spot. I miss her every minute of the day, and no one knows how often I think of her; whenever I do, my eyes fill with tears. Moortje is so sweet, and I love her so much that I keep dreaming she'll come back to us.

I have plenty of dreams, but the reality is that we'll have to stay here until the war is over. We can't ever go outside, and the only visitors we can have are Miep, her husband Jan, Bep Voskuijl, Mr Voskuijl, Mr Kugler, Mr Kleiman and Mrs Kleiman, though she hasn't come because she thinks it's too dangerous.

COMMENT ADDED BY ANNE IN SEPTEMBER 1942: *Daddy's always so nice. He understands me perfectly, and I wish we could have a heart-to-heart talk sometime without my bursting instantly into tears. But apparently that has to do with my age. I'd like to spend all my time writing, but that would probably get boring.*

Up till now I've only confided my thoughts to my diary.
I still haven't got round to writing amusing sketches that I
could read aloud at a later date. In the future I'm going to
devote less time to sentimentality and more time to reality.

Dear Kitty,

I've deserted you for an entire month, but so little has happened that I can't find a newsworthy item to relate every single day. The van Daans arrived on 13 July. We thought they were coming on the fourteenth, but from the thirteenth to sixteenth the Germans were sending out call-up notices right and left and causing a lot of unrest, so they decided it would be safer to leave a day too early than a day too late.

Peter van Daan arrived at nine-thirty in the morning (while we were still at breakfast). Peter's going on sixteen, a shy, awkward boy whose company won't amount to much. Mr and Mrs van Daan came half an hour later. Much to our amusement, Mrs van Daan was carrying a hatbox with a large chamber pot inside. 'I just don't feel at home without my chamber pot,' she exclaimed, and it was the first item to find a permanent place under the divan. Instead of a chamber pot, Mr van D. was lugging a collapsible tea table under his arm.

From the first, we ate our meals together, and after three days it felt as if the seven of us had become one big family. Naturally, the van Daans had much to tell about the week we'd been away from civilization. We were especially interested in what had happened to our flat and to Mr Goldschmidt.

Mr van Daan filled us in: 'Monday morning at nine, Mr Goldschmidt phoned and asked if I could come over. I went straightaway and found a very distraught Mr Goldschmidt.

He showed me a note that the Frank family had left behind. As instructed, he was planning to take the cat to the neighbours, which I agreed was a good idea. He was afraid the house was going to be searched, so we went through all the rooms, tidying up here and there and clearing the breakfast things off the table. Suddenly I saw a notepad on Mrs Frank's desk, with an address in Maastricht written on it. Even though I knew Mrs Frank had left it on purpose, I pretended to be surprised and horrified and begged Mr Goldschmidt to burn this incriminating piece of paper. I swore up and down that I knew nothing about your disappearance, but that the note had given me an idea. "Mr Goldschmidt," I said, "I bet I know what this address refers to. About six months ago a high-ranking officer came to the office. It seems he and Mr Frank grew up together. He promised to help Mr Frank if it was ever necessary. As I recall, he was stationed in Maastricht. I think this officer has kept his word and is somehow planning to help them cross over to Belgium and then to Switzerland. There's no harm in telling this to any friends of the Franks who come asking about them. Of course, you don't need to mention the part about Maastricht." And after that I left. This is the story most of your friends have been told, because I heard it later from several other people.'

We thought it was extremely funny, but we laughed even harder when Mr van Daan told us that certain people have vivid imaginations. For example, one family living on our square claimed they saw all four of us riding by on our bikes early in the morning, and another woman was absolutely positive we'd been loaded into some kind of military vehicle in the middle of the night.

Yours, Anne

Dear Kitty,

Now our Secret Annexe has truly become secret. Because so many houses are being searched for hidden bicycles, Mr Kugler thought it would be better to have a bookcase built in front of the entrance to our hiding place. It swings out on its hinges and opens like a door. Mr Voskuijl did the carpentry work. (Mr Voskuijl has been told that the seven of us are in hiding, and he's been most helpful.)

Now whenever we want to go downstairs we have to duck and then jump. After the first three days we were all walking around with bumps on our foreheads from banging our heads against the low doorway. Then Peter cushioned it by nailing a towel stuffed with wood shavings to the door frame. Let's see if it helps!

I'm not doing much schoolwork. I've given myself a holiday until September. Father wants to start giving me lessons then, but we have to buy all the books first.

There's little change in our lives here. Peter's hair was washed today, but that's nothing special. Mr van Daan and I are always at loggerheads with each other. Mummy always treats me like a baby, which I can't stand. For the rest, things are going better. I don't think Peter's got any nicer. He's an obnoxious boy who lies around on his bed all day, only rousing himself to do a little carpentry work before returning to his nap. What a clot!

Mummy gave me another one of her dreadful sermons this morning. We take the opposite view on everything. Daddy's a sweetheart; he may get cross with me, but it never lasts longer than five minutes.

It's a beautiful day outside, nice and hot, and in spite of

everything, we make the most of the weather by lounging on the folding bed in the attic.

Yours, Anne

COMMENT ADDED BY ANNE ON 21 SEPTEMBER 1942: *Mr van Daan has been as nice as pie to me recently. I've said nothing, but have been enjoying it while it lasts.*

WEDNESDAY, 2 SEPTEMBER 1942

Dearest Kitty,

Mr and Mrs van Daan have had a terrible argument. I've never seen anything like it, since Mother and Father wouldn't dream of shouting at each other like that. The argument was based on something so trivial it didn't seem worth wasting a single word on it. Oh well, to each his own.

Of course, it's very difficult for Peter, who gets caught in the middle, but no one takes Peter seriously any more, since he's hypersensitive and lazy. Yesterday he was beside himself with worry because his tongue was blue instead of pink. This rare phenomenon disappeared as quickly as it came. Today he's walking around with a thick scarf on because he's got a stiff neck. His Highness has been complaining of lumbago too. Aches and pains in his heart, kidneys and lungs are also par for the course. He's an absolute hypochondriac! (That's the right word, isn't it?)

Mother and Mrs van Daan aren't getting along very well. There are enough reasons for the friction. To give you one small example, Mrs van D. has removed all but three of her sheets from our communal linen cupboard. She's assuming that Mother's can be used for both families. She'll be in for a nasty surprise when she discovers that Mother has followed her lead.

Furthermore, Mrs van D. is miffed because we're using her china instead of ours. She's still trying to find out what we've done with our plates; they're a lot closer than she thinks, since they're packed in cardboard boxes in the attic, behind a load of Opekta advertising material. As long as we're in hiding, the plates will remain out of her reach. Since I'm always having accidents, it's just as well! Yesterday I broke one of Mrs van D.'s soup bowls.

'Oh!' she angrily exclaimed. 'Can't you be more careful? That was my last one.'

Please bear in mind, Kitty, that the two ladies speak abominable Dutch (I don't dare comment on the gentlemen: they'd be highly insulted). If you were to hear their bungled attempts, you'd laugh your head off. We've given up pointing out their errors, since correcting them doesn't help anyway. Whenever I quote Mother or Mrs van Daan, I'll write proper Dutch instead of trying to duplicate their speech.

Last week there was a brief interruption in our monotonous routine. This was provided by Peter – and a book about women. I should explain that Margot and Peter are allowed to read nearly all the books Mr Kleiman lends us. But the adults preferred to keep this special book to themselves. This immediately piqued Peter's curiosity. What forbidden fruit did it contain? He sneaked off with it when his mother was downstairs talking, and took himself and his booty to the loft. For two days all was well. Mrs van Daan knew what he was up to, but kept mum until Mr van Daan found out about it. He threw a fit, took the book away and assumed that would be the end of the business. However, he'd neglected to take his son's curiosity into account. Peter, not in the least fazed by his father's swift action, began thinking up ways to read the rest of this vastly interesting book.

In the meantime, Mrs van D. asked Mother for her opinion. Mother didn't think this particular book was suitable for Margot, but she saw no harm in letting her read most other books.

'You see, Mrs van Daan,' Mother said, 'there's a big difference between Margot and Peter. To begin with, Margot's a girl, and girls are always more mature than boys. Second, she's already read many serious books and doesn't go looking for those which are no longer forbidden. Third, Margot's much more sensible and intellectually advanced, as a result of her four years at an excellent school.'

Mrs van Daan agreed with her, but felt it was wrong as a matter of principle to let youngsters read books written for adults.

Meanwhile, Peter had thought of a suitable time when no one would be interested in either him or the book. At seven-thirty in the evening, when the entire family was listening to the wireless in the private office, he took his treasure and stole off to the loft again. He should have been back by eight-thirty, but he was so engrossed in the book that he forgot the time and was just coming down the stairs when his father entered the room. The scene that followed was not surprising: after a slap, a whack and a tug-of-war, the book lay on the table and Peter was in the loft.

This is how matters stood when it was time for the family to eat. Peter stayed upstairs. No one gave him a moment's thought; he'd have to go to bed without his dinner. We continued eating, chatting merrily away, when suddenly we heard a piercing whistle. We lay down our forks and stared at each other, the shock clearly visible on our pale faces.

Then we heard Peter's voice through the chimney: 'I won't come down!'

Mr van Daan leapt up, his napkin falling to the floor, and shouted, with the blood rushing to his face, 'I've had enough!'

Father, afraid of what might happen, grabbed him by the arm and the two men went to the attic. After much struggling and kicking, Peter ended up in his room with the door shut, and we went on eating.

Mrs van Daan wanted to save a piece of bread for her darling son, but Mr van D. was adamant. 'If he doesn't apologize this minute, he'll have to sleep in the loft.'

We protested that going without dinner was enough punishment. What if Peter were to catch cold? We wouldn't be able to call a doctor.

Peter didn't apologize, and returned to the loft. Mr van Daan decided to leave well enough alone, though he did note the next morning that Peter's bed had been slept in. At seven Peter went to the attic again, but was persuaded to come downstairs when Father spoke a few friendly words to him. After three days of sullen looks and stubborn silence, everything was back to normal.

Yours, Anne

MONDAY, 21 SEPTEMBER 1942

Dearest Kitty,

Today I'll tell you the general news here in the Annexe. A lamp has been mounted above my divan bed so that in future, when I hear the guns going off, I'll be able to pull a cord and switch on the light. I can't use it at the moment because we're keeping our window open a little, day and night.

The male members of the van Daan contingent have built

a very handy wood-stained food safe, with real screens. Up till now this glorious cupboard has been located in Peter's room, but in the interests of fresh air it's been moved to the attic. Where it once stood, there's now a shelf. I advised Peter to put his table underneath the shelf, add a nice rug and hang his own cupboard where the table now stands. That might make his little cubbyhole more comfy, though I certainly wouldn't like to sleep there.

Mrs van Daan is unbearable. I'm continually being scolded for my incessant chatter when I'm upstairs. I simply let the words bounce right off me! Madame now has a new trick up her sleeve: trying to get out of washing the pots and pans. If there's a bit of food left at the bottom of the pan, she leaves it to spoil instead of transferring it to a glass dish. Then in the afternoon when Margot is stuck with cleaning all the pots and pans, Madame exclaims, 'Oh, poor Margot, you have so much work to do!'

Every other week Mr Kleiman brings me a couple of books written for girls my age. I'm enthusiastic about the *Joop ter Heul* series. I've enjoyed all of Cissy van Marxveldt's books very much. I've read *The Zaniest Summer* four times, and the ludicrous situations still make me laugh.

Father and I are currently working on our family tree, and he tells me something about each person as we go along.

I've begun my schoolwork. I'm working hard at French, cramming five irregular verbs into my head every day. But I've forgotten much too much of what I learned in school.

Peter has taken up his English with great reluctance. A few schoolbooks have just arrived, and I brought a large supply of exercise-books, pencils, rubbers and labels from home. Pim (that's our pet name for Father) wants me to help him with his Dutch lessons. I'm perfectly willing to teach him in exchange for his assistance with French and other subjects. But he makes the most unbelievable mistakes!

I sometimes listen to the Dutch broadcasts from London. Prince Bernhard recently announced that Princess Juliana is expecting a baby in January, which I think is wonderful. No one here understands why I take such an interest in the Royal Family.

A few nights ago I was the topic of discussion, and we all decided I was an ignoramus. As a result, I threw myself into my schoolwork the next day, since I have little desire to still be in the first form when I'm fourteen or fifteen. The fact that I'm hardly allowed to read anything was also discussed. At the moment, Mother's reading *Gentlemen, Wives and Servants*, and of course I'm not allowed to read it (though Margot is!). First I have to be more intellectually developed, like my genius of a sister. Then we discussed my ignorance of philosophy, psychology and physiology (I immediately looked up these big words in the dictionary!). It's true, I don't know anything about these subjects. But maybe I'll have learned more by next year!

I've come to the shocking conclusion that I have only one long-sleeved dress and three cardigans to wear in the winter. Father's given me permission to knit a white jumper; the wool isn't very pretty, but it'll be warm, and that's what counts. Some of our clothing was left with friends, but unfortunately we won't be able to get to it until after the war. Provided it's still there, of course.

I'd just finished writing something about Mrs van Daan when she walked into the room. Thump, I slammed the book shut.

'Hey, Anne, can't I even take a peek?'

'No, Mrs van Daan.'

'Just the last page then?'

'No, not even the last page, Mrs van Daan.'

Of course, I nearly died, since that particular page contained a rather unflattering description of her.

There's something happening every day, but I'm too tired and lazy to write it all down.

Yours, Anne

FRIDAY, 25 SEPTEMBER 1942

Dearest Kitty,

Father has a friend, a man in his mid-seventies named Mr Dreher, who's sick, poor and deaf as a post. At his side, like a useless appendage, is his wife, twenty-seven years younger and equally poor, whose arms and legs are loaded with real and fake bracelets and rings left over from more prosperous days. This Mr Dreher has already been a great nuisance to Father, and I've always admired the saintly patience with which he handled this pathetic old man on the phone. When we were still living at home, Mother used to advise him to put a gramophone in front of the receiver, one that would repeat every three minutes, 'Yes, Mr Dreher' and 'No, Mr Dreher', since the old man never understood a word of Father's lengthy replies anyway.

Today Mr Dreher phoned the office and asked Mr Kugler to come and see him. Mr Kugler wasn't in the mood and said he would send Miep, but Miep cancelled the appointment. Mrs Dreher called the office three times, but since Miep was reportedly out the entire afternoon, she had to imitate Bep's voice. Downstairs in the office as well as upstairs in the Annexe, there was great hilarity. Now each time the phone rings, Bep says 'That's Mrs Dreher!' and Miep has to laugh, so that the people on the other end of the line are greeted with an impolite giggle. Can't you just picture it? This has got to be the greatest office in the whole wide world. The bosses and the office girls have such fun together!

Some evenings I go to the van Daans for a little chat. We eat 'mothball biscuits' (biscuits that were stored in a wardrobe that was mothproofed) and have a good time. Recently the conversation was about Peter. I said that he often pats me on the cheek, which I don't like. They asked me in a typically grown-up way whether I could ever learn to love Peter like a brother, since he loves me like a sister. 'Oh, no!' I said, but what I was thinking was, 'Oh, ugh!' Just imagine! I added that Peter's a bit stiff, perhaps because he's shy. Boys who aren't used to being around girls are like that.

I must say that the Annexe Committee (the men's section) is very creative. Listen to the scheme they've come up with to get a message to Mr Broks, an Opekta Co. sales representative and friend who's surreptitiously hidden some of our things for us! They're going to type a letter to a shop owner in southern Zeeland who is, indirectly, one of Opekta's customers and ask him to fill out a form and send it back in the enclosed self-addressed envelope. Father will write the address on the envelope himself. Once the letter is returned from Zeeland, the form can be removed and a handwritten message confirming that Father is alive can be inserted in the envelope. This way Mr Broks can read the letter without suspecting a ruse. They chose the province of Zeeland because it's close to Belgium (a letter can easily be smuggled across the border) and because no one is allowed to travel there without a special permit. An ordinary salesman like Mr Broks would never be granted a permit.

Yesterday Father put on another act. Groggy with sleep,

he stumbled off to bed. His feet were cold, so I lent him my bed socks. Five minutes later he flung them to the floor. Then he pulled the blankets over his head because the light bothered him. The lamp was switched off, and he gingerly poked his head out from under the covers. It was all very amusing. We started talking about the fact that Peter says Margot is a 'busy bee'. Suddenly Daddy's voice was heard from the depths: 'A busybody, you mean.'

Mouschi, the cat, is becoming nicer to me as time goes by, but I'm still somewhat afraid of her.

Yours, Anne

SUNDAY, 27 SEPTEMBER 1942

Dearest Kitty,

Mother and I had a so-called 'discussion' today, but the annoying part is that I burst into tears. I can't help it. Daddy is *always* nice to me, and he also understands me much better. At moments like these I can't stand Mother. It's obvious that I'm a stranger to her; she doesn't even know what I think about the most ordinary things.

We were talking about maids and the fact that you're supposed to refer to them as 'domestic help' these days. She claimed that when the war is over, that's what they'll want to be called. I didn't quite see it that way. Then she added that I talk about 'later' so often and that I act as if I were such a lady, even though I'm not, but I don't think building sand-castles in the air is such a terrible thing to do, as long as you don't take it too seriously. At any rate, Daddy usually comes to my defence. Without him I wouldn't be able to stick it out here.

I don't get along with Margot very well either. Even though our family never has the same kind of outbursts they have upstairs, I find it far from pleasant. Margot's and Mother's personalities are so alien to me. I understand my girlfriends better than my own mother. Isn't that a shame?

For the umpteenth time, Mrs van Daan is sulking. She's very moody and has been removing more and more of her belongings and locking them up. It's too bad Mother doesn't repay every van Daan 'disappearing act' with a Frank 'disappearing act'.

Some people, like the van Daans, seem to take special delight not only in raising their own children but in helping others raise theirs. Margot doesn't need it, since she's naturally good, kind and clever, perfection itself, but I seem to have enough mischief for the two of us. More than once the air has been filled with the van Daans' admonitions and my cheeky replies. Father and Mother always defend me fiercely. Without them I wouldn't be able to jump back into the fray with my usual composure. They keep telling me I should talk less, mind my own business and be more modest, but I seem doomed to failure. If Father weren't so patient, I'd have long ago given up hope of ever meeting my parents' quite moderate expectations.

If I take a small helping of a vegetable I loathe and eat potatoes instead, the van Daans, especially Mrs van Daan, can't get over how spoiled I am. 'Come on, Anne, eat some more vegetables,' she says.

'No, thank you, ma'am,' I reply. 'The potatoes are more than enough.'

'Vegetables are good for you; your mother says so too. Have some more,' she insists, until Father intervenes and upholds my right to refuse a dish I don't like.

Then Mrs van D. really flies off the handle: 'You should have been at our house, where children were brought up the way they should be. I don't call this a proper upbringing.

Anne is terribly spoiled. I'd never allow that. If Anne were my daughter . . .'

This is always how her tirades begin and end: 'If Anne were my daughter . . .' Thank goodness I'm not.

But to get back to the subject of raising children, yesterday a silence fell after Mrs van D. finished her little speech. Father then replied, 'I think Anne is very well brought up. At least she's learned not to respond to your interminable sermons. As far as the vegetables are concerned, all I have to say is look who's calling the kettle black.'

Mrs van D. was soundly defeated. The pot calling the kettle black refers of course to Madame herself, since she can't tolerate beans or any kind of cabbage in the evening because they give her 'wind'. But I could say the same. What a twit, don't you think? In any case, let's hope she stops talking about me.

It's so funny to see how quickly Mrs van Daan flushes. I don't, and it secretly annoys her no end.

Yours, Anne

MONDAY, 28 SEPTEMBER 1942

Dearest Kitty,

I had to stop yesterday, though I was nowhere near finished. I'm dying to tell you about another one of our clashes, but before I do I'd like to say this: I think it's odd that grown-ups quarrel so easily and so often and about such petty matters. Up till now I always thought bickering was just something children did and that they outgrew it. Of course, there's sometimes a reason to have a 'real' quarrel, but the verbal exchanges that take place here are just plain bickering. I should be used to the fact that these squabbles are daily occurrences, but I'm not and never will be as long as I'm the subject of nearly every discussion. (They refer to these as 'discussions' instead of 'quarrels', but Germans don't know the difference!) They criticize everything, and I mean everything, about me: my behaviour, my personality, my manners; every inch of me, from head to toe and back again, is the subject of gossip and debate. Harsh words and shouts are constantly being flung at my head, though I'm absolutely not used to it. According to the powers that be, I'm supposed to grin and bear it. But I can't! I have no intention of taking their insults lying down. I'll show them that Anne Frank wasn't born yesterday. They'll sit up and take notice and keep their big mouths shut when I make them see they ought to attend to their own manners instead of mine. How dare they behave like that! It's simply barbaric. I've been astonished, time and again, at such rudeness and most of all . . . at such stupidity (Mrs van Daan). But as soon as I've got used to the idea, and that shouldn't take long, I'll give them a taste of their own medicine, and then they'll change their tune! Am I really as bad-mannered, headstrong, stubborn, pushy, stupid, lazy, etc., etc., as the van Daans say I am? No, of course not. I know I have my faults and shortcomings, but they blow them all out of proportion! If you only knew, Kitty, how I seethe when they scold and mock me. It won't take long before I explode with pent-up rage.

But enough of that. I've bored you long enough with my quarrels, and yet I can't resist adding a highly interesting dinner conversation.

Somehow we landed on the subject of Pim's extreme diffidence. His modesty is a well-known fact, which even the stupidest person wouldn't dream of questioning. All of a sudden Mrs van Daan, who feels the need to bring herself into every conversation, remarked, 'I'm very modest and retiring too, much more so than my husband!'

Have you ever heard anything so ridiculous? This sentence clearly illustrates that she's not exactly what you'd call modest!

Mr van Daan, who felt obliged to explain the 'much more so than my husband', answered calmly, 'I have no desire to be modest and retiring. In my experience, you get a lot further by being pushy!' And turning to me, he added, 'Don't be modest and retiring, Anne. It will get you nowhere.'

Mother agreed completely with this viewpoint. But, as usual, Mrs van Daan had to add her two penn'orth. This time, however, instead of addressing me directly, she turned to my parents and said, 'You must have a strange outlook on life to be able to say that to Anne. Things were different when I was growing up. Though they probably haven't changed much since then, except in your modern household!'

This was a direct hit at Mother's modern child-rearing methods, which she's defended on many occasions. Mrs van Daan was so upset her face turned bright red. People who flush easily become even more agitated when they feel themselves getting hot under the collar, and they quickly lose to their opponents.

The non-flushed mother, who now wanted to have the matter over and done with as quickly as possible, paused for a moment to think before she replied. 'Well, Mrs van Daan, I agree that it's much better if a person isn't over-modest. My husband, Margot and Peter are all exceptionally modest. Your husband, Anne and I, though not exactly the opposite, don't let ourselves be pushed around.'

Mrs van Daan: 'Oh, but Mrs Frank, I don't understand what you mean! Honestly, I'm extremely modest and retiring. How can you say that I'm pushy?'

Mother: 'I didn't say you were pushy, but no one would describe you as having a retiring disposition.'

Mrs van D.: 'I'd like to know in what way I'm pushy! If I didn't look out for myself here, no one else would, and I'd soon starve, but that doesn't mean I'm not as modest and retiring as your husband.'

Mother had no choice but to laugh at this ridiculous self-defence, which irritated Mrs van Daan. Not exactly a born debater, she continued her magnificent account in a mixture of German and Dutch, until she got so tangled up in her own words that she finally rose from her chair and was just about to leave the room when her eye fell on me. You should have seen her! As luck would have it, the moment Mrs van D. turned around I was shaking my head in a combination of compassion and irony. I wasn't doing it on purpose, but I'd followed her tirade so intently that my reaction was completely involuntary. Mrs van D. wheeled around and gave me a tongue-lashing: hard, Germanic, mean and vulgar, exactly like some fat, red-faced fishwife. It was a joy to behold. If I could draw, I'd like to have sketched her as she was then. She struck me as so comical, that silly little scatterbrain! I've learned one thing: you only really get to know a person after a row. Only then can you judge their true character!

Yours, Anne

TUESDAY, 29 SEPTEMBER 1942

Dearest Kitty,

The strangest things happen to you when you're in hiding! Try to picture this. Because we don't have a bath, we wash ourselves in a tin tub, and because there's only hot water in the office (by which I mean the entire lower floor), the seven of us take turns making the most of this great opportunity. But since no two of us are alike and we are all plagued by varying degrees of modesty, each member of the family has selected a different place to wash. Peter takes a bath in the office kitchen, even though it has a glass door. When it's time for his bath, he goes round to each of us in turn and announces that we shouldn't walk past the kitchen for the next half hour. He considers this measure to be sufficient. Mr van D. takes his bath upstairs, reasoning that the safety of his own room outweighs the difficulty of having to carry the hot water up all those stairs. Mrs van D. has yet to take a bath; she's waiting to see which is the best place. Father washes in the private office and Mother in the kitchen behind a fireguard, while Margot and I have declared the front office to be our bathing grounds. Since the curtains are drawn on Saturday afternoon, we scrub ourselves in the dark, while the one who isn't in the bath looks out of the window through a chink in the curtains and gazes in wonder at the endlessly amusing people.

A week ago I decided I didn't like this spot and have been on the lookout for more comfortable quarters. It was Peter who gave me the idea of setting my tin bath in the spacious office lavatory. I can sit down, turn on the light, lock the door, pour out the water without anyone's help, and all without the fear of being seen. I used my lovely bathroom for the first time on Sunday and, strange as it may seem, I like it better than any other place.

The plumber was at work downstairs on Wednesday, moving the water pipes and drains from the office lavatory to the passage so the pipes won't freeze during a cold winter. The plumber's visit was far from pleasant. Not only were we not allowed to run water during the day, but the lavatory was also out of bounds. I'll tell you how we handled this problem; you may find it unseemly of me to bring it up, but I'm not so prudish about matters of this kind. On the day of our arrival, Father and I improvised a chamber pot, sacrificing a preserving jar for this purpose. For the duration of the plumber's visit, preserving jars were put into service during the daytime to hold our calls of nature. As far as I was concerned, this wasn't half as difficult as having to sit still all day and not say a word. You can imagine how hard that was for Miss Quack, Quack, Quack. On ordinary days we have to speak in a whisper; not being able to talk or move at all is ten times worse.

After three days of constant sitting, my backside was stiff and sore. Nightly calisthenics helped.

Yours, Anne

THURSDAY, 1 OCTOBER 1942

Dear Kitty,

Yesterday I had a horrible fright. At eight o'clock the doorbell suddenly rang. All I could think of was that someone was coming to get us, you know who I mean. But I calmed down when everybody swore it must have been either pranksters or the postman.

The days here are very quiet. Mr Levinsohn, a little Jewish chemist, is doing some experiments for Mr Kugler in the kitchen. Since he's familiar with the entire building, we're in constant dread that he'll take it into his head to go and have a look at what used to be the laboratory. We're as still as baby mice. Who would have guessed three months ago that quicksilver Anne would have to sit so quietly for hours on end, and what's more, that she could?

Mrs van Daan's birthday was the twenty-ninth. Though we didn't have a large celebration, she was showered with flowers, simple gifts and good food. Apparently the red carnations from her spouse are a family tradition.

Let me pause a moment on the subject of Mrs van Daan and tell you that her attempts to flirt with Father are a constant source of irritation to me. She pats him on the cheek and head, pulls up her skirt and makes so-called witty remarks in an effort to get Pim's attention. Fortunately, he finds her neither pretty nor charming, so he doesn't respond to her flirtations. As you know, I'm quite the jealous type, and I can't abide her behaviour. After all, Mother doesn't act that way towards Mr van D., which is what I told Mrs van D. right to her face.

From time to time Peter can be very amusing. He and I have one thing in common: we like to dress up, which makes everyone laugh. One evening we made our appearance, with Peter in one of his mother's skin-tight dresses and me in his suit. He wore a hat; I had a cap on. The grown-ups split their sides laughing, and we enjoyed ourselves every bit as much.

Bep bought new skirts for Margot and me at The Bijenkorf. The fabric is hideous, like the sacks that potatoes come in. Just the kind of thing the department stores wouldn't dare sell in the olden days, now costing 24.00 guilders (Margot's) and 7.75 guilders (mine).

We have a nice treat in store: Bep's ordered a correspondence course in shorthand for Margot, Peter and me. Just you wait, by this time next year we'll be able to take perfect shorthand. In any case, learning to write a secret code like that is really interesting.

I have a terrible pain in my index finger (on my left hand), so I can't do any ironing. What luck!

Mr van Daan wants me to sit next to him at the table, since Margot doesn't eat enough to suit him. That's all right with me, I like changes. There's always a tiny black cat roaming around the yard, and it reminds me of my dear sweet Moortje. Another reason I welcome the change is that Mummy's always carping at me, especially at the table. Now Margot will have to bear the brunt of it. Or rather, won't, since Mother doesn't make such sarcastic remarks to her. Not to that paragon of virtue! I'm always teasing Margot about being a paragon of virtue these days, and she hates it. Maybe it'll teach her not to be such a goody-goody. High time she learned.

To end this hodgepodge of news, a particularly amusing joke told by Mr van Daan:

What goes click ninety-nine times and clack once?
A centipede with a clubfoot.

Bye-bye, Anne

SATURDAY, 3 OCTOBER 1942

Dear Kitty,

Everybody teased me quite a bit yesterday because I lay down on the bed next to Mr van Daan. 'At your age! Shocking!' and other remarks along those lines. Silly, of course. I'd never want to sleep with Mr van Daan the way they mean.

Yesterday Mother and I had another run-in and she really kicked up a fuss. She told Daddy all my sins and started to cry, which made me cry too, and I already had such an awful headache. I finally told Daddy that I love 'him' more than I do Mother, to which he replied that it was just a passing phase, but I don't think so. I simply can't stand Mother, and I have to force myself not to snap at her all the time, and to stay calm, when I'd rather slap her across the face. I don't know why I've taken such a terrible dislike to her. Daddy says that if Mother isn't feeling well or has a headache, I should volunteer to help her, but I'm not going to because I don't love her and don't enjoy doing it. I can imagine Mother dying someday, but Daddy's death seems inconceivable. It's very mean of me, but that's how I feel. I hope Mother will *never* read this or anything else I've written.

I've been allowed to read more grown-up books lately. *Eva's Youth* by Nico van Suchtelen is currently keeping me busy. I don't think there's much of a difference between this and books for teenage girls. Eva thought that children grew on trees, like apples, and that the stork plucked them off the tree when they were ripe and brought them to the mothers. But her girlfriend's cat had kittens and Eva saw them coming out of the cat, so she thought cats laid eggs and hatched them like chickens, and that mothers who wanted a child also went upstairs a few days before their time to lay an egg and brood on it. After the babies arrived, the mothers were pretty weak from all that squatting. At some point, Eva wanted a baby too. She took a woollen scarf and spread it on the ground so the egg could fall into it, and then she squatted down and began to push. She clucked as she waited, but no egg came out. Finally, after she'd been sitting for a long time, something did come, but it was a sausage instead of an egg. Eva was embarrassed. She thought she was ill. Funny, isn't it? There are also parts of *Eva's Youth* that talk about women selling their bodies on the street and asking loads of money. I'd be mortified in front of a man like that. In addition, it mentions Eva's menstruation. Oh, I long to have my period – then I'll really be grown up.

Daddy is grumbling again and threatening to take away my diary. Oh, horror of horrors! From now on, I'm going to hide it.

Anne Frank

I imagine that . . .

I've gone to Switzerland. Daddy and I sleep in one room, while the boys'* study is turned into a sitting-room, where I can receive visitors. As a surprise, they've bought new furniture for me, including a tea table, a desk, armchairs and a divan. Everything's simply wonderful. After a few days Daddy gives me 150 guilders – converted into Swiss money, of course, but I'll call them guilders – and tells me to buy everything I think I'll need, all for myself. (Later on, I get a guilder a week, which I can also use to buy whatever I want.) I set off with Bernd and buy:

3 cotton vests @ 0.50 = 1.50
3 cotton knickers @ 0.50 = 1.50
3 wool vests @ 0.75 = 2.25
3 wool knickers @ 0.75 = 2.25
2 petticoats @ 0.50 = 1.00
2 bras (smallest size) @ 0.50 = 1.00
5 pyjamas @ 1.00 = 5.00
1 light dressing-gown @ 2.50 = 2.50
1 thick dressing-gown @ 3.00 = 3.00
2 bed jackets @ 0.75 = 1.50
1 small pillow @ 1.00 = 1.00
1 pair of lightweight slippers @ 1.00 = 1.00
1 pair of warm slippers @ 1.50 = 1.50
1 pair of summer shoes (school) @ 1.50 = 1.50
1 pair of summer shoes (best) @ 2.00 = 2.00
1 pair of winter shoes (school) @ 2.50 = 2.50
1 pair of winter shoes (best) @ 3.00 = 3.00

---

* Anne's cousins Bernhard (Bernd) and Stephan Elias.

2 aprons @ 0.50 = 1.00
25 handkerchiefs @ 0.05 = 1.25
4 pairs of silk stockings @ 0.75 = 3.00
4 pairs of kneesocks @ 0.50 = 2.00
4 pairs of socks @ 0.25 = 1.00
2 pairs of thick stockings @ 1.00 = 2.00
3 skeins of white wool (underwear, cap) = 1.50
3 skeins of blue wool (sweater, skirt) = 1.50
3 skeins of variegated wool (cap, scarf) = 1.50
Scarves, belts, collars, buttons = 1.25

Plus 2 school dresses (summer), 2 school dresses (winter), 2 good dresses (summer), 2 good dresses (winter), 1 summer skirt, 1 good winter skirt, 1 school winter skirt, 1 raincoat, 1 summer coat, 1 winter coat, 2 hats, 2 caps. For a total of 108.00 guilders.

2 handbags, 1 ice-skating outfit, 1 pair of skates, 1 case (containing powder, skin cream, foundation cream, cleansing cream, suntan lotion, cotton wool, first-aid kit, rouge, lipstick, eyebrow pencil, bath salts, bath powder, eau-de-Cologne, soap, powder puff).

Plus 4 sweaters @ 1.50, 4 blouses @ 1.00, miscellaneous items @ 10.00 and books, presents @ 4.50.

FRIDAY, 9 OCTOBER 1942

Dearest Kitty,

Today I have nothing but dismal and depressing news to report. Our many Jewish friends and acquaintances are being taken away in droves. The Gestapo is treating them very roughly and transporting them in cattle-trucks to Westerbork, the big camp in Drenthe to which they're sending all the

Jews. Miep told us about someone who'd managed to escape from there. It must be terrible in Westerbork. The people get almost nothing to eat, much less to drink, as water is available only one hour a day, and there's only one lavatory and sink for several thousand people. Men and women sleep in the same room, and women and children often have their heads shaved. Escape is almost impossible; many people look Jewish, and they're branded by their shorn heads.

If it's that bad in Holland, what must it be like in those faraway and uncivilized places where the Germans are sending them? We assume that most of them are being murdered. The English radio says they're being gassed. Perhaps that's the quickest way to die.

I feel terrible. Miep's accounts of these horrors are so heartrending, and Miep is also very distraught. The other day, for instance, the Gestapo deposited an elderly, crippled Jewish woman on Miep's doorstep while they set off to find a car. The old woman was terrified of the glaring searchlights and the guns firing at the English planes overhead. Yet Miep didn't dare let her in. Nobody would. The Germans are generous enough when it comes to punishment.

Bep is also very subdued. Her boyfriend is being sent to Germany. Every time the planes fly over, she's afraid they're going to drop their entire bomb load on Bertus's head. Jokes like 'Oh, don't worry, they can't all fall on him' or 'One bomb is all it takes' are hardly appropriate in this situation. Bertus is not the only one being forced to work in Germany. Trainloads of young men depart daily. Some of them try to sneak off the train when it stops at a small station, but only a few manage to escape unnoticed and find a place to hide.

But that's not the end of my lamentations. Have you ever heard the term 'hostages'? That's the latest punishment for saboteurs. It's the most horrible thing you can imagine.

Leading citizens – innocent people – are taken prisoner to await their execution. If the Gestapo can't find the saboteur, they simply grab five hostages and line them up against the wall. You read the announcements of their death in the paper, where they're referred to as 'fatal accidents'.

Fine specimens of humanity, those Germans, and to think I'm actually one of them! No, that's not true, Hitler took away our nationality long ago. And besides, there are no greater enemies on earth than the Germans and the Jews.

Yours, Anne

WEDNESDAY, 14 OCTOBER 1942

Dear Kitty,

I'm terribly busy. Yesterday I began by translating a chapter from *La Belle Nivernaise* and writing down vocabulary words. Then I worked on an *awful* maths problem and translated three pages of French grammar besides. Today, French grammar and history. I simply refuse to do that wretched maths every day. Daddy thinks it's awful too. I'm almost better at it than he is, though in fact neither of us is any good, so we always have to call on Margot's help. I'm also working away at my shorthand, which I enjoy. Of the three of us, I've made the most progress.

I've read *The Storm Family*. It's quite good, but doesn't compare with *Joop ter Heul*. Anyway, the same words can be found in both books, which makes sense because they're written by the same author. Cissy van Marxveldt is a terrific writer. I'm definitely going to let my own children read her books too.

Moreover, I've read a lot of Körner plays. I like the way he writes. For example, *Hedwig*, *The Cousin from Bremen*, *The Governess*, *The Green Domino*, etc.

Mother, Margot and I are once again the best of friends. It's actually a lot nicer that way. Last night Margot and I were lying side by side in my bed. It was incredibly cramped, but that's what made it fun. She asked if she could read my diary once in a while.

'Parts of it,' I said, and asked about hers. She gave me permission to read her diary as well.

The conversation turned to the future, and I asked what she wanted to be when she was older. But she wouldn't say and was quite mysterious about it. I gathered it had something to do with teaching; of course, I'm not absolutely sure, but I suspect it's something along those lines. I really shouldn't be so nosy.

This morning I lay on Peter's bed, after first having chased him off it. He was furious, but I didn't care. He might consider being a little more friendly to me from time to time. After all, I did give him an apple last night.

I once asked Margot if she thought I was ugly. She said that I was okay and had nice eyes. A little vague, don't you think?

Well, until next time!

Anne Frank

PS. This morning we all took turns on the scale. Margot now weighs 9 stone 6 pounds, Mother 9 stone 10, Father 11 stone 1, Anne 6 stone 12, Peter 10 stone 8, Mrs van Daan 8 stone 5, Mr van Daan 11 stone 11. In the three months since I've been here, I've gained 19 pounds. A lot, huh?

TUESDAY, 20 OCTOBER 1942

Dearest Kitty,

My hand's still shaking, though it's been two hours since we had the scare. I should explain that there are five fire extinguishers in the building. The office staff stupidly forgot to warn us that the carpenter, or whatever he's called, was coming to fill the extinguishers. As a result, we didn't bother to be quiet until I heard the sound of hammering on the landing (across from the bookcase). I immediately assumed it was the carpenter and went to warn Bep, who was eating lunch, that she couldn't go back downstairs. Father and I stationed ourselves at the door so we could hear when the man had left. After working for about fifteen minutes, he laid his hammer and some other tools on our bookcase (or so we thought!) and banged on our door. We turned white with fear. Had he heard something after all and did he now want to check out this mysterious-looking bookcase? It seemed so, since he kept knocking, pulling, pushing and jerking on it.

I was so scared I nearly fainted at the thought of this total stranger managing to discover our wonderful hiding place. Just when I thought my days were numbered, we heard Mr Kleiman's voice saying, 'Open up, it's me.'

We opened the door at once. What had happened? The hook fastening the bookcase had got stuck, which is why no one had been able to warn us about the carpenter. After the man had left, Mr Kleiman came to get Bep, but couldn't open the bookcase. I can't tell you how relieved I was. In my imagination, the man I thought was trying to get inside the Secret Annexe had kept growing and growing until he'd become not only a giant but also the cruellest Fascist in the world. Whew. Fortunately, everything worked out all right, at least this time.

We had lots of fun on Monday. Miep and Jan spent the night with us. Margot and I slept in Father and Mother's room for the night so the Gieses could have our beds. The menu was drawn up in their honour, and the meal was delicious. The festivities were briefly interrupted when

Father's lamp caused a short circuit and we were suddenly plunged into darkness. What were we to do? We did have fuses, but the fuse box was at the rear of the dark warehouse, which made this a particularly unpleasant job at night. Still, the men ventured forth, and ten minutes later we were able to put away the candles.

I was up early this morning. Jan was already dressed. Since he had to leave at eight-thirty, he was upstairs eating breakfast by eight. Miep was busy getting dressed, and I found her in her vest when I came in. She wears the same kind of long underwear I do when she cycles. Margot and I threw on our clothes as well and were upstairs earlier than usual. After a pleasant breakfast, Miep headed downstairs. It was pouring outside and she was glad she didn't have to cycle to work. Daddy and I made the beds, and afterwards I learned five irregular French verbs. Quite industrious, don't you think?

Margot and Peter were reading in our room, with Mouschi curled up beside Margot on the divan. After my irregular French verbs, I joined them and read *The Woods Are Singing for All Eternity*. It's quite a beautiful book, but very unusual. I'm almost finished.

Next week it's Bep's turn to spend the night.

Yours, Anne

THURSDAY, 29 OCTOBER 1942

My dearest Kitty,

I'm very worried. Father's ill. He's covered with spots and has a high temperature. It looks like measles. Just think, we can't even call a doctor! Mother is making him perspire in hopes of sweating out the fever.

This morning Miep told us that the furniture has been

removed from the van Daans' flat on Zuider-Amstel-laan. We haven't told Mrs van D. yet. She's been so '*nerven-mässig*'* lately, and we don't feel like hearing her moan and groan again about all the beautiful china and lovely chairs she had to leave behind. We had to abandon most of our nice things too. What's the good of grumbling about it now?

Father wants me to start reading books by Hebbel and other well-known German writers. I can read German fairly well by now, except that I usually mumble the words instead of reading them silently to myself. But that'll pass. Father has taken the plays of Goethe and Schiller down from the big bookcase and is planning to read to me every evening. We've started off with *Don Carlos*. Encouraged by Father's good example, Mother pressed her prayer book into my hands. I read a few prayers in German, just to be polite. They certainly sound beautiful, but they mean very little to me. Why is she making me act so religious and devout?

Tomorrow we're going to light the stove for the first time. The chimney hasn't been swept in ages, so the room is bound to fill with smoke. Let's hope the thing draws!

Yours, Anne

MONDAY, 2 NOVEMBER 1942

Dear Kitty,

Bep stayed with us Friday evening. It was fun, but she didn't sleep very well because she'd drunk some wine. For the rest, there's nothing special to report. I had an awful headache yesterday and went to bed early. Margot's being exasperating again.

---

* Nervous.

This morning I began sorting out an index card file from the office, because it'd fallen over and got all mixed up. Before long I was going barmy. I asked Margot and Peter to help, but they were too lazy, so I put it away. I'm not crazy enough to do it all by myself!

Anne Frank

PS. I forgot to mention the important news that I'm probably going to have my period soon. I can tell because I keep finding a whitish smear in my panties, and Mother predicted it would start soon. I can hardly wait. It's such a momentous event. Too bad I can't use sanitary towels, but you can't get them any more, and Mummy's tampons can be used only by women who've had a baby.

COMMENT BY ANNE ON 22 JANUARY 1944:
I wouldn't be able to write that kind of thing any more.

Now that I'm rereading my diary after a year and a half, I'm surprised at my childish innocence. Deep down I know I could never be that innocent again, however much I'd like to be. I can understand the mood changes and the comments about Margot, Mother and Father as if I'd written them only yesterday, but I can't imagine writing so openly about other matters. It embarrasses me greatly to read the pages dealing with subjects that I remembered as being nicer than they actually were. My descriptions are so indelicate. But enough of that.

I can also understand my homesickness and yearning for Moortje. The whole time I've been here I've longed unconsciously – and at times consciously – for trust, love and physical affection. This longing may change in intensity, but it's always there.

Dear Kitty,

The British have finally scored a few successes in Africa and Stalingrad hasn't fallen yet, so the men are happy and we had coffee and tea this morning. For the rest, nothing special to report.

This week I've been reading a lot and doing little work. That's the way things ought to be. That's surely the road to success.

Mother and I are getting along better lately, but we're *never* close. Father's not very open about his feelings, but he's the same sweetheart he's always been. We lit the stove a few days ago and the entire room is still filled with smoke. I prefer central heating, and I'm probably not the only one. Margot's a stinker (there's no other word for it), a constant source of irritation, morning, noon and night.

Anne Frank

Dearest Kitty,

Mother's nerves are very much on edge, and that doesn't bode well for me. Is it just a coincidence that Father and Mother never scold Margot and always blame me for everything? Last night, for example, Margot was reading a book with beautiful illustrations; she got up and put the book aside for later. I wasn't doing anything, so I picked it up and began looking at the pictures. Margot came back, saw 'her' book in my hands, knitted her brow and crossly demanded the book back. I wanted to look through it a bit more. Margot got angrier by the minute, and Mother butted in: 'Margot was reading that book; give it back to her.'

Father came in, and without even knowing what was going on, saw that Margot was being wronged and lashed out at me: 'I'd like to see what you'd do if Margot was looking at one of your books!'

I promptly gave in, put the book down and, according to them, left the room 'in a huff'. I was neither huffy nor cross, but merely sad.

It wasn't right of Father to pass judgement without knowing what the issue was. I would have given the book to Margot myself, and a lot sooner, if Father and Mother hadn't intervened and rushed to take Margot's part, as if she were suffering some great injustice.

Of course, Mother took Margot's side; they always take each other's sides. I'm so used to it that I've become completely indifferent to Mother's rebukes and Margot's moodiness. I love them, but only because they're Mother and Margot. I don't give a dash about them as people. As far as I'm concerned, they can go jump in the lake. It's different with Father. When I see him being partial to Margot, approving Margot's every action, praising her, hugging her, I feel a gnawing ache inside, because I'm mad about him. I model myself on Father, and there's no one in the world I love more. He doesn't realize that he treats Margot differently from me: Margot just happens to be the cleverest, the kindest, the prettiest and the best. But I have a right to be taken seriously too. I've always been the clown and mischief-maker of the family; I've always had to pay double for my sins: once with scoldings and then again with my own sense of despair. I'm no longer satisfied with the meaningless affection or the supposedly serious talks. I long for something from Father that he's incapable of giving. I'm not jealous of Margot; I never have been. I'm not envious of her brains or her beauty. It's just that I'd like to feel that Father really loves me, not because I'm his child, but because I'm me, Anne.

I cling to Father because my contempt of Mother is growing daily and it's only through him that I'm able to retain the last ounce of family feeling I have left. He doesn't understand that I sometimes need to vent my feelings for Mother. He doesn't want to talk about it, and he avoids any discussion involving Mother's failings.

And yet Mother, with all her shortcomings, is tougher for me to deal with. I don't know how I should behave. I can't very well confront her with her carelessness, her sarcasm and her hard-heartedness, yet I can't continue to take the blame for everything.

I'm the opposite of Mother, so of course we clash. I don't mean to judge her; I don't have that right. I'm simply looking at her as a mother. She's not a mother to me – I have to mother myself. I've cut myself adrift from them. I'm charting my own course, and we'll see where it leads me. I have no choice, because I can picture what a mother and a wife should be and can't seem to find anything of the sort in the woman I'm supposed to call 'Mother'.

I tell myself time and again to overlook Mother's bad example. I only want to see her good points, and to look inside myself for what's lacking in her. But it doesn't work, and the worst part is that Father and Mother don't realize their own inadequacies and how much I blame them for letting me down. Are there any parents who can make their children completely happy?

Sometimes I think God is trying to test me, both now and in the future. I'll have to become a good person on my own, without anyone to serve as a model or advise me, but it'll make me stronger in the end.

Who else but me is ever going to read these letters? Who else but me can I turn to for comfort? I'm frequently in need of consolation, I often feel weak, and more often than not, I fail to meet expectations. I know this, and every day I resolve to do better.

They aren't consistent in their treatment of me. One day they say that Anne's a sensible girl and entitled to know everything, and the next that Anne's a silly noodle who doesn't know a thing and yet imagines she's learned all she needs to know from books! I'm no longer the baby and spoiled little darling whose every deed can be laughed at. I have my own ideas, plans and ideals, but am unable to articulate them yet.

Oh well. So much comes into my head at night when I'm alone, or during the day when I'm obliged to put up with people I can't abide or who invariably misinterpret my intentions. That's why I always come back to my diary – I start there and end there because Kitty's always patient. I promise her that, despite everything, I'll keep going, that I'll find my own way and choke back my tears. I only wish I could see some results or, just once, receive encouragement from someone who loves me.

Don't condemn me, but think of me as a person who sometimes reaches bursting point!

Yours, Anne

Dearest Kitty,

Yesterday was Peter's birthday, his sixteenth. I was upstairs by eight, and Peter and I looked at his presents. He received a game of Monopoly, a razor and a cigarette lighter. Not that he smokes so much, not at all; it just looks so distinguished.

The biggest surprise came from Mr van Daan, who reported at one that the English had landed in Tunis, Algiers, Casablanca and Oran.

'This is the beginning of the end,' everyone was saying, but Churchill, the British Prime Minister, who must have heard the same thing being repeated in England, declared, 'This is not the end. It is not even the beginning of the end. But it is, perhaps, the end of the beginning.' Do you see the difference? However, there's reason for optimism. Stalingrad, the Russian city that has been under attack for three months, still hasn't fallen into German hands.

In the true spirit of the Annexe, I should talk to you about food. (I should explain that they're real gluttons up on the top floor.)

Bread is delivered daily by a very nice baker, a friend of Mr Kleiman's. Of course, we don't have as much as we did at home, but it's enough. We also purchase ration books on the black market. The price keeps going up; it's already risen from 27 to 33 guilders. And that for mere sheets of printed paper!

To provide ourselves with a source of nutrition that will keep, aside from the hundred tins of food we've stored here, we bought three hundred pounds of beans. Not just for us, but for the office staff as well. We'd hung the sacks of beans on hooks in the hallway, just inside our secret entrance, but a few seams split under the weight. So we decided to move them to the attic, and Peter was entrusted with the heavy lifting. He managed to get five of the six sacks upstairs intact and was busy with the last one when the sack broke and a flood, or rather a hailstorm, of brown beans went flying through the air and down the stairs. Since there were about fifty pounds of beans in that sack, it made enough noise to raise the dead. Downstairs they were sure the house was falling down around their heads. Peter was stunned, but then burst into peals of laughter when he saw me standing at the bottom of the stairs, like an island in a sea of brown, with waves of beans lapping at my ankles. We promptly began picking them up, but beans are so small and slippery that they roll into every conceivable corner and hole. Now each time we go upstairs, we bend over and hunt around so we can present Mrs van Daan with a handful of beans.

I almost forgot to mention that Father has recovered from his illness.

Yours, Anne

PS. The radio has just announced that Algiers has fallen. Morocco, Casablanca and Oran have been in British hands for several days. We're now waiting for Tunis.

TUESDAY, 10 NOVEMBER 1942

Dearest Kitty,

Great news! We're planning to take an eighth person into hiding with us!

Yes, really. We always thought there was enough room and food for one more person, but we were afraid of placing an even greater burden on Mr Kugler and Mr Kleiman. But since reports of the dreadful things being done to the Jews are getting worse by the day, Father decided to sound out these two gentlemen, and they thought it was an excellent plan. 'It's just as dangerous, whether there are seven or eight,' they noted rightly. Once this was settled, we sat down and mentally went through our circle of acquaintances, trying to come up with a single person who would blend in well with our extended family. This wasn't difficult. After Father had rejected all the van Daan relatives, we chose a dentist named Albert Dussel. He lives with a charming Christian lady who's quite a bit younger than he is. They're probably not married, but that's beside the point. He's known to be quiet and refined, and he seemed, from our superficial acquaintance with him, to be nice. Miep knows him as well, so she'll be able to make the necessary arrangements. If he comes, Mr Dussel will have to sleep in my room instead of Margot, who will have to make do with the folding bed.* We'll ask him to bring along something to fill cavities with.

Yours, Anne

THURSDAY, 12 NOVEMBER 1942

Dearest Kitty,

Miep came to tell us that she'd been to see Dr Dussel. He asked her the moment she entered the room if she knew of a hiding place and was enormously pleased when Miep said she had something in mind. She added that he'd need to go into hiding as soon as possible, preferably Saturday, but he thought this was highly improbable, since he wanted to bring his records up to date, settle his accounts and attend to a couple of patients. Miep relayed the message to us this morning. We didn't think it was wise to wait so long. All

---

* After Dussel arrived, Margot slept in her parents' bedroom.

these preparations require explanations to various people who we feel ought to be kept in the dark. Miep went to ask if Dr Dussel couldn't manage to come on Saturday after all, but he said no, and now he's scheduled to arrive on Monday.

I think it's odd that he doesn't jump at our proposal. If they pick him up on the street, it won't help either his records or his patients, so why the delay? If you ask me, it's stupid of Father to humour him.

Otherwise, no news.

Yours, Anne

TUESDAY, 17 NOVEMBER 1942

Dearest Kitty!

Mr Dussel has arrived. Everything went smoothly. Miep told him to be at a certain place in front of the post office at 11.00 a.m., when a man would meet him, and he was at the appointed place at the appointed time. Mr Kleiman went up to him, announced that the man he was expecting to meet was unable to come and asked him to drop by the office to see Miep. Mr Kleiman took a tram back to the office while Mr Dussel followed on foot.

It was eleven-twenty when Mr Dussel tapped on the office door. Miep asked him to remove his coat, so the yellow star couldn't be seen, and brought him to the private office, where Mr Kleiman kept him occupied until the cleaning lady had gone. On the pretext that the private office was needed for something else, Miep took Mr Dussel upstairs, opened the bookcase and stepped inside, while Mr Dussel looked on in amazement.

In the meantime, the seven of us had seated ourselves around the dining-table to await the latest addition to our family with coffee and cognac. Miep first led him into the Frank family's room. He immediately recognized our furniture, but had no idea we were upstairs, just above his head. When Miep told him, he was so astonished he nearly fainted. Thank goodness she didn't leave him in suspense any longer, but brought him upstairs. Mr Dussel sank into a chair and stared at us in dumbstruck silence, as though he thought he could read the truth on our faces. Then he stuttered, '*Aber* . . . but are you *nicht* in Belgium? The officer, the auto, they were not coming? Your escape was not working?'

We explained the whole thing to him, about how we'd deliberately spread the rumour of the officer and the car to throw the Germans and anyone else who might come looking for us off the track. Mr Dussel was speechless in the face of such ingenuity, and could do nothing but gaze around in surprise as he explored the rest of our lovely and ultra-practical Annexe. We all had lunch together. Then he had a short nap, joined us for tea, put away the few belongings Miep had been able to bring here in advance and began to feel much more at home. Especially when we handed him the following typewritten rules and regulations for the Secret Annexe (a van Daan production):

PROSPECTUS AND GUIDE TO THE SECRET ANNEXE

A Unique Facility for the Temporary Accommodation of Jews and Other Dispossessed Persons

Open all year round: Located in beautiful, quiet, wooded surroundings in the heart of Amsterdam. No private residences in the vicinity. Can be reached by trams 13 or 17 and also by car and bicycle. For those to whom such transport has been forbidden by the

German authorities, it can also be reached on foot. Furnished and unfurnished rooms and apartments are available at all times, with or without meals.

Price: Free.

Diet: Low-fat.

Running water in the bathroom (sorry, no bath) and on various inside and outside walls. Cosy stoves for heating.

Ample storage space for a variety of goods. Two large, modern safes.

Private radio with a direct line to London, New York, Tel Aviv and many other stations. Available to all residents after 6.00 p.m. No listening to forbidden broadcasts, with certain exceptions, i.e. German stations may only be tuned in to listen to classical music. It is absolutely forbidden to listen to German news bulletins (regardless of where they are transmitted from) and to pass them on to others.

Rest hours: From 10.00 p.m. to 7.30 a.m.; 10.15 a.m. on Sundays. Owing to circumstances, residents are required to observe rest hours during the daytime when instructed to do so by the Management. To ensure the safety of all, rest hours must be strictly observed!!!

Free-time activities: None allowed outside the house until further notice.

Use of language: It is necessary to speak softly at all times. Only the language of civilized people may be spoken, thus no German.

Reading and relaxation: No German books may be read, except for the classics and works of a scholarly nature. Other books are optional.

Calisthenics: Daily.

Singing: Only softly, and after 6.00 p.m.

Films: Prior arrangements required.

Lessons: A weekly correspondence course in short-hand. Courses in English, French, maths and history offered at any hour of the day or night. Payment in the form of tuition, e.g. Dutch.

Separate department for the care of small household pets (with the exception of vermin, for which special permits are required).

Mealtimes:

Breakfast: At 9.00 a.m. daily except public holidays and Sundays; at approximately 11.30 a.m. on Sundays and public holidays.

Lunch: A light meal. From 1.15 p.m. to 1.45 p.m.

Dinner: May or may not be a hot meal. Mealtime depends on news broadcasts.

Obligations with respect to the Supply Corps: Residents must be prepared to help with office work at all times.

Baths: The tin bath is available to all residents after 9.00 a.m. on Sundays. Residents may wash in the downstairs lavatory, kitchen, private office or front office, as they choose.

Alcohol: For medicinal purposes only.

The end.

Yours, Anne

THURSDAY, 19 NOVEMBER 1942

Dearest Kitty,

Just as we thought, Mr Dussel is a very nice man. Of course he didn't mind sharing a room with me; to be honest, I'm not exactly delighted at having a stranger use my things, but you have to make sacrifices for a good cause, and I'm glad I can make this small one. 'If we can save even one of our friends, the rest doesn't matter,' said Father, and he's absolutely right.

The first day Mr Dussel was here, he asked me all sorts of questions – for example, what time the cleaning lady comes to the office, how we've arranged to use the bathroom and when we're allowed to go to the lavatory. You may laugh, but these things aren't so easy in a hiding place. During the daytime we can't make any noise that might be heard downstairs, and when someone else is there, like the cleaning lady, we have to be extra careful. I patiently explained all this to Mr Dussel, but I was surprised to see how slow he is to catch on. He asks everything twice and still can't remember what you've told him.

Maybe he's just confused by the sudden change and he'll get over it. Otherwise, everything is fine.

Mr Dussel has told us much about the outside world we've missed for so long. He had sad news. Countless friends and acquaintances have been taken off to a dreadful fate. Night after night, green and grey military vehicles cruise the streets. They knock on every door, asking whether any Jews live there. If so, the whole family is immediately taken away. If not, they proceed to the next house. It's impossible to escape their clutches unless you go into hiding. They often go around with lists, knocking only on those doors where they know there's a big haul to be made. They frequently offer a bounty, so much per head. It's like the slave hunts of the olden days. I don't mean to make light of this; it's much too tragic for that. In the evenings when it's dark, I often see long lines of good, innocent people, accompanied by crying children, walking on and on, ordered about by a handful of men who bully and beat them until they nearly drop. No one is spared. The sick, the elderly, children, babies and pregnant women – all are marched to their death.

We're so fortunate here, away from the turmoil. We wouldn't have to give a moment's thought to all this suffering if it weren't for the fact that we're so worried about those we hold dear, whom we can no longer help. I feel wicked sleeping in a warm bed, while somewhere out there my dearest friends are dropping from exhaustion or being knocked to the ground.

I get frightened myself when I think of close friends who are now at the mercy of the cruellest monsters ever to stalk the earth.

And all because they're Jews.

Yours, Anne

FRIDAY, 20 NOVEMBER 1942

Dearest Kitty,

We don't really know how to react. Up till now very little news about the Jews had reached us here, and we thought it best to stay as cheerful as possible. Every now and then Miep used to mention what had happened to a friend, and Mother or Mrs van Daan would start to cry, so she decided it was better not to say any more. But we bombarded Mr Dussel with questions, and the stories he had to tell were so gruesome and dreadful that we can't get them out of our heads. Once we've had time to digest the news, we'll probably go back to our usual joking and teasing. It won't do us or those outside any good if we continue to be as gloomy as we are now. And what would be the point of turning the Secret Annexe into a Melancholy Annexe?

No matter what I'm doing, I can't help thinking about those who are gone. I catch myself laughing and remember that it's a disgrace to be so cheerful. But am I supposed to spend the whole day crying? No, I can't do that. This gloom will pass.

Added to this misery there's another, but of a more personal nature, and it pales in comparison to the suffering I've just told you about. Still, I can't help telling you that lately I've begun to feel deserted. I'm surrounded by too great a void. I never used to give it much thought, since my mind was filled with my friends and having a good time. Now I think either about unhappy things or about myself. It's taken a while, but I've finally realized that Father, no matter how kind he may be, can't take the place of my former world. When it comes to my feelings, Mother and Margot ceased to count long ago.

But why do I bother you with this foolishness? I'm terribly ungrateful, Kitty, I know, but when I've been scolded for the umpteenth time and have all these other woes to think about as well, my head begins to reel!

Yours, Anne

SATURDAY, 28 NOVEMBER 1942

Dearest Kitty,

We've been using too much electricity and have now exceeded our ration. The result: excessive economy and the prospect of having the electricity cut off. No light for a fortnight; that's a pleasant thought, isn't it? But who knows, maybe it won't be so long! It's too dark to read after four or four-thirty, so we while away the time with all kinds of crazy activities: telling riddles, doing calisthenics in the dark, speaking English or French, reviewing books – after a while everything gets boring. Yesterday I discovered a new pastime: using a good pair of binoculars to peek into the lighted rooms of the neighbours. During the day our curtains can't be opened, not even an inch, but there's no harm when it's so dark.

I never knew that neighbours could be so interesting. Ours are, at any rate. I've come across a few at dinner, one family making a cine-film and the dentist opposite working on a frightened old lady.

Mr Dussel, the man who was said to get along so well with children and to absolutely adore them, has turned out to be an old-fashioned disciplinarian and preacher of unbearably long sermons on manners. Since I have the singular pleasure (!) of sharing my far too narrow room with His Excellency, and since I'm generally considered to be the worst behaved of the three young people, it's all I can do to avoid having the same old scoldings and admonitions repeatedly flung at my head and to pretend not to hear. This wouldn't be so bad if Mr Dussel weren't such a telltale and hadn't singled out Mother to be the recipient of his reports. If Mr Dussel's just read me the riot act, Mother lectures me all over again, this time throwing the whole book at me. And if I'm really lucky, Mrs van D. calls me to account five minutes later and lays down the law as well!

Really, it's not easy being the badly brought-up centre of attention of a family of nit-pickers.

In bed at night, as I ponder my many sins and exaggerated shortcomings, I get so confused by the sheer amount of things I have to consider that I either laugh or cry, depending on my mood. Then I fall asleep with the strange feeling of wanting to be different from what I am or being different from what I want to be, or perhaps of behaving differently from what I am or want to be.

Oh dear, now I'm confusing you too. Forgive me, but I don't like crossing things out, and in these times of scarcity, tossing away a piece of paper is clearly taboo. So I can only advise you not to reread the above passage and to make no attempt to get to the bottom of it, because you'll never find your way out again!

Yours, Anne

Dearest Kitty,

Hanukkah and St Nicholas' Day nearly coincided this year; they were only one day apart. We didn't make much of a fuss with Hanukkah, merely exchanging a few small gifts and lighting the candles. Since candles are in short supply, we lit them for only ten minutes, but as long as we sing the song, that doesn't matter. Mr van Daan made a menorah out of wood, so that was taken care of too.

St Nicholas' Day on Saturday was much more fun. During dinner Bep and Miep were so busy whispering to Father that our curiosity was aroused and we suspected they were up to something. Sure enough, at eight o'clock we all trooped downstairs through the passage in pitch darkness (it gave me the shivers, and I wished I was safely back upstairs!) to the alcove. We could switch on the light, since this room doesn't have any windows. When that was done, Father opened the big cupboard.

'Oh, how wonderful!' we all cried.

In the corner was a large basket decorated with colourful paper and a mask of Black Peter.

We quickly took the basket upstairs with us. Inside was a little gift for everyone, including an appropriate verse. Since you're familiar with the kinds of poems people write each other on St Nicholas' Day, I won't copy them down for you.

I received a doll, Father got bookends, and so on. Well anyway, it was a nice idea, and since the eight of us had never celebrated St Nicholas' Day before, this was a good time to begin.

Yours, Anne

PS. We also had presents for everyone downstairs, a few things left over from the Good Old Days; plus Miep and Bep are always grateful for money.

Today we heard that Mr van Daan's ashtray, Mr Dussel's picture frame and Father's bookends were made by none other than Mr Voskuijl. How anyone can be so clever with his hands is a mystery to me!

THURSDAY, 10 DECEMBER 1942

Dearest Kitty,

Mr van Daan used to be in the meat, sausage and spice business. He was hired for his knowledge of spices, and yet, to our great delight, it's his sausage talents that have come in handy now.

We ordered a large amount of meat (under the counter, of course) that we were planning to preserve in case there were hard times ahead. Mr van Daan decided to make bratwurst, sausages and mettwurst. I had fun watching him put the meat through the mincer: once, twice, three times. Then he added the remaining ingredients to the minced meat and used a long pipe to force the mixture into the casings. We ate the bratwurst with sauerkraut for lunch, but the sausages, which were going to be preserved, had to dry first, so we hung them over a pole suspended from the ceiling. Everyone who came into the room burst into laughter when they saw the dangling sausages. It was such a comical sight.

The kitchen was a shambles. Mr van Daan, clad in his wife's apron and looking fatter than ever, was working away at the meat. What with his bloody hands, red face and spotted apron, he looked like a real butcher. Mrs van D. was trying to do everything at once: learning Dutch out of a book, stirring the soup, watching the meat, sighing and moaning about her broken rib. That's what happens when old (!) ladies do such stupid exercises to get rid of their fat behinds! Dussel had an eye infection and was sitting next to the stove dabbing his eye with camomile tea. Pim, seated in the one ray of sunshine coming through the window, kept having to move his chair this way and that to stay out of the way. His rheumatism must have been bothering him because he was slightly hunched over and was keeping an eye on Mr van Daan with an agonized expression on his face. He reminded me of those aged invalids you see in the poorhouse. Peter was romping around the room with Mouschi, the cat, while Mother, Margot and I were peeling boiled potatoes. When you get right down to it, none of us was doing our work properly, because we were all so busy watching Mr van Daan.

Dussel has opened his dental practice. Just for fun, I'll describe the session with his very first patient.

Mother was ironing, and Mrs van D., the first victim, sat down on a chair in the middle of the room. Dussel, unpacking his case with an air of importance, asked for some eau-de-Cologne, which could be used as a disinfectant, and Vaseline, which would have to do for wax. He looked in Mrs van D.'s mouth and found two teeth that made her wince with pain and utter incoherent cries every time he touched them. After a lengthy examination (lengthy as far as Mrs van D. was concerned, since it actually took no longer than two minutes), Dussel began to scrape out a cavity. But Mrs van D. had no intention of letting him. She flailed her arms and legs until Dussel finally let go of his probe and . . . it remained stuck in Mrs van D.'s tooth. That really did it! Mrs van D. lashed out wildly in all directions, cried (as much as you can with an instrument like that in your mouth), tried to remove it, but only managed to push it in even farther. Mr Dussel calmly observed the scene, his hands on his hips, while the rest of the audience roared with laughter. Of course, that was very mean of us. If it'd been me, I'm sure I would have yelled even louder. After a great deal of squirming, kicking, screaming and shouting, Mrs van D. finally managed to yank the thing out, and Mr Dussel went on with his work as if nothing had happened. He was so quick that Mrs van D. didn't have time to pull any more shenanigans. But then, he had more help than he's ever had before: no fewer than two assistants; Mr van D. and I performed our job well. The whole scene resembled one of those engravings from the Middle Ages entitled 'A Quack at Work'. In the meantime, however, the patient was getting restless, since she had to keep an eye on 'her' soup and 'her' food. One thing is certain: it'll be a while before Mrs van D. makes another dental appointment!

Yours, Anne

SUNDAY, 13 DECEMBER 1942

Dearest Kitty,

I'm sitting here nice and cosy in the front office, peering out through a chink in the heavy curtains. It's dark, but there's just enough light to write by.

It's really strange watching people walk past. They all seem to be in such a hurry that they nearly trip over their own feet. Those on bicycles whiz by so fast I can't even tell who's on the bike. The people in this neighbourhood aren't particularly attractive to look at. The children especially are so dirty you wouldn't want to touch them with a bargepole. Real slum kids with runny noses. I can hardly understand a word they say.

Yesterday afternoon, when Margot and I were taking a bath, I said, 'What if we took a fishing rod and reeled in each of those kids one by one as they walked by, stuck them in the tub, washed and mended their clothes and then . . .'

'And then tomorrow they'd be just as dirty and tattered as they were before,' Margot replied.

But I'm babbling. There are also other things to look at: cars, boats and the rain. I can hear the tram and the children and I'm enjoying myself.

Our thoughts are subject to as little change as we are. They're like a merry-go-round, turning from the Jews to food, from food to politics. By the way, speaking of Jews, I saw two yesterday when I was peeking through the curtains. I felt as though I were gazing at one of the Seven Wonders of the World. It gave me such a funny feeling, as if I'd denounced them to the authorities and was now spying on their misfortune.

Opposite us is a houseboat. The captain lives there with his wife and children. He has a small yapping dog. We know the little dog only by its bark and by its tail, which we can see whenever it runs round the deck. Oh, what a shame, it's just started raining and most of the people are hidden under their umbrellas. All I can see are raincoats, and now and again the back of a stocking-capped head. Actually, I don't even need to look. By now I can recognize the women at a glance: gone to fat from eating potatoes, dressed in a red or green coat and worn-out shoes, a shopping bag dangling from their arms, with faces that are either grim or good-humoured, depending on the mood of their husbands.

Yours, Anne

Dearest Kitty,

The Annexe was delighted to hear that we'll all be receiving an extra quarter of a pound of butter for Christmas. According to the newspaper, everyone is entitled to half a pound, but they mean those lucky souls who get their ration books from the government, not Jews in hiding like us who can only afford to buy four rather than eight ration books on the black market. Each of us is going to bake something with the butter. This morning I made two cakes and some biscuits. It's very busy upstairs, and Mother has informed me that I'm not to do any studying or reading until all the household tasks have been finished.

Mrs van Daan is lying in bed nursing her bruised rib. She complains all day long, constantly demands that the bandages be changed and is generally dissatisfied with everything. I'll be glad when she gets back on her feet and can clean up after herself because, I must admit, she's extraordinarily hardworking and neat, and as long as she's in good physical and mental condition, she's quite cheerful.

As if I don't hear 'shh, shh' enough during the day because I'm always making 'too much' noise, my dear room-mate has come up with the idea of saying 'shh, shh' to me all night too. According to him, I shouldn't even turn over. I refuse to take any notice of him, and the next time he shushes me, I'm going to shush him right back.

He gets more exasperating and egotistical as the days go by. Except for the first week, I haven't seen even one of the biscuits he so generously promised me. He's particularly infuriating on Sundays, when he switches on the light at the crack of dawn to exercise for ten minutes.

To me, the torment seems to last for hours, since the chairs I use to make my bed longer are constantly being jiggled under my sleepy head. After rounding off his limbering-up exercises with a few vigorous arm swings, His Lordship begins dressing. His underwear is hanging on a hook, so first he lumbers over to get it and then lumbers back, past my bed. But his tie is on the table, so once again he pushes and bumps his way past the chairs.

But I mustn't waste any more of your time griping about disgusting old men. It won't help matters anyway. My plans for revenge, such as unscrewing the light bulb, locking the door and hiding his clothes, have unfortunately had to be abandoned in the interests of peace.

Oh, I'm becoming so sensible! We've got to be reasonable about everything we do here: studying, listening, holding our tongues, helping others, being kind, making compromises and I don't know what else! I'm afraid my common sense, which was in short supply to begin with, will be used up too quickly and I won't have any left by the time the war is over.

Yours, Anne

WEDNESDAY, 13 JANUARY 1943

Dearest Kitty,

This morning I was constantly interrupted, and as a result I haven't been able to finish a single thing I've begun.

We have a new pastime, namely, filling packets with powdered gravy. The gravy is one of Gies & Co.'s products. Mr Kugler hasn't been able to find anyone else to fill the packets, and besides, it's cheaper if we do the job. It's the kind of work they do in prisons. It's incredibly boring and makes us dizzy and giggly.

Terrible things are happening outside. At any time of night and day, poor helpless people are being dragged out of their homes. They're allowed to take only a rucksack and a little cash with them, and even then, they're robbed of these possessions on the way. Families are torn apart; men, women and children are separated. Children come home from school to find that their parents have disappeared. Women return from shopping to find their houses sealed, their families gone. The Christians in Holland are also living in fear because their sons are being sent to Germany. Everyone is scared. Every night hundreds of planes pass over Holland on their way to German cities, to sow their bombs on German soil. Every hour hundreds, or maybe even thousands, of people are being killed in Russia and Africa. No one can keep out of the conflict, the entire world is at war, and even though the Allies are doing better, the end is nowhere in sight.

As for us, we're quite fortunate. Luckier than millions of people. It's quiet and safe here, and we're using our money to buy food. We're so selfish that we talk about 'after the war' and look forward to new clothes and shoes, when actually we should be saving every penny to help others when the war is over, to salvage whatever we can.

The children in this neighbourhood run around in thin shirts and wooden clogs. They have no coats, no socks, no caps and no one to help them. Gnawing on a carrot to still their hunger pangs, they walk from their cold houses through cold streets to an even colder classroom. Things have got so bad in Holland that hordes of children stop passers-by in the streets to beg for a piece of bread.

I could spend hours telling you about the suffering the war has brought, but I'd only make myself more miserable. All we can do is wait, as calmly as possible, for it to end. Jews and Christians alike are waiting, the whole world is waiting, and many are waiting for death.

Yours, Anne

SATURDAY, 30 JANUARY 1943

Dearest Kitty,

I'm seething with rage, yet I can't show it. I'd like to scream, stamp my foot, give Mother a good shaking, cry and I don't know what else because of the nasty words, mocking looks and accusations that she hurls at me day after day, piercing me like arrows from a tightly strung bow, which are nearly impossible to pull from my body. I'd like to scream at Mother, Margot, the van Daans, Dussel and Father too: 'Leave me alone, let me have at least one night when I don't cry myself to sleep with my eyes burning and my head pounding. Let me get away, away from everything, away from this world!' But I can't do that. I can't let them see my doubts, or the wounds they've inflicted on me. I couldn't bear their sympathy or their good-humoured derision. It would only make me want to scream even more.

Everyone thinks I'm showing off when I talk, ridiculous when I'm silent, insolent when I answer, cunning when I have a good idea, lazy when I'm tired, selfish when I eat one bite more than I should, stupid, cowardly, calculating, etc., etc. All day long I hear nothing but what an exasperating child I am, and although I laugh it off and pretend not to mind, I do mind. I wish I could ask God to give me another personality, one that doesn't antagonize everyone.

But that's impossible. I'm stuck with the character I was born with, and yet I'm sure I'm not a bad person. I do my best to please everyone, more than they'd ever suspect in a million years. When I'm upstairs, I try to laugh it off because I don't want them to see my troubles.

More than once, after a series of absurd reproaches, I've snapped at Mother: 'I don't care what you say. Why don't you just wash your hands of me – I'm a hopeless case.' Of course, she'd tell me not to talk back and virtually ignore me for two days. Then suddenly all would be forgotten and she'd treat me like everyone else.

It's impossible for me to be all smiles one day and venomous the next. I'd rather choose the golden mean, which isn't so golden, and keep my thoughts to myself. Perhaps sometime I'll treat the others with the same contempt as they treat me. Oh, if only I could.

Yours, Anne

Dearest Kitty,

Though it's been ages since I've written to you about the squabbles, there's still no change. In the beginning Mr Dussel took our soon-forgotten clashes very seriously, but now he's grown used to them and no longer tries to mediate.

Margot and Peter aren't exactly what you'd call 'young'; they're both so quiet and boring. Next to them, I stick out like a sore thumb, and I'm always being told, 'Margot and Peter don't act that way. Why don't you follow your sister's example!' I hate that.

I confess that I have absolutely no desire to be like Margot. She's too weak-willed and passive to suit me; she lets herself be swayed by others and always gives way under pressure.

I want to have more backbone! But I keep ideas like these to myself. They'd only laugh at me if I offered this in my defence.

During meals the air is filled with tension. Fortunately, the outbursts are sometimes held in check by the 'soup eaters', the people from the office who come up to have a cup of soup for lunch.

This afternoon Mr van Daan again brought up the fact that Margot eats so little. 'I suppose you do it to keep your figure,' he added in a mocking tone.

Mother, who always comes to Margot's defence, said in a loud voice, 'I can't stand that stupid chatter of yours a minute longer.'

Mrs van D. turned red as a beetroot. Mr van D. stared straight ahead and said nothing.

Still, we often have a good laugh. Not long ago Mrs van D. was entertaining us with some bit of nonsense or other. She was talking about the past, about how well she got along with her father and what a flirt he was. 'And you know,' she continued, 'my father told me that if a gentleman ever got fresh, I was to say, "Remember, sir, that I'm a lady," and he'd know what I meant.' We split our sides laughing, as if she'd told us a good joke.

Even Peter, though he's usually quiet, occasionally gives rise to hilarity. He has the misfortune of adoring foreign words without knowing what they mean. One afternoon we couldn't use the lavatory because there were visitors in the office. Unable to wait, he went to the toilet but didn't flush it. To warn us of the unpleasant smell, he tacked a sign to the door: 'RSVP – gas!'. Of course, he meant 'Danger – gas!' but he thought 'RSVP' looked more elegant. He didn't have the faintest idea that it meant 'please reply'.

Yours, Anne

Dearest Kitty,

Pim is expecting the invasion any day now. Churchill has had pneumonia, but is gradually getting better. Gandhi, the champion of Indian freedom, is on one of his umpteenth hunger strikes.

Mrs van D. claims she's fatalistic. But who's the most afraid when the guns go off? None other than Petronella van Daan.

Jan brought along the episcopal letter that the bishops addressed to their parishioners. It was beautiful and inspiring. 'People of the Netherlands, stand up and take action. Each of us must choose our own weapons to fight for the freedom of our country, our people and our religion! Give your help and support. Act now!' This is what they're preaching from the pulpit. Will it do any good? It's definitely too late to help our fellow Jews.

Guess what's happened to us now? The owner of the building sold it without informing Mr Kugler and Mr Kleiman. One morning the new landlord arrived with an architect to look the place over. Thank goodness Mr Kleiman was in the office. He showed the gentlemen all there was to see, with the exception of the Secret Annexe. He claimed he'd left the key at home and the new owner asked no further questions. If only he doesn't come back demanding to see the Annexe. In that case, we'll be in big trouble!

Father emptied a card file for Margot and me and filled it with index cards that are blank on one side. This is to become our reading file, in which Margot and I are supposed to note down the books we've read, the author and the date. I've learned two new words: 'brothel' and 'coquette'. I've bought a separate exercise-book for new words.

There's a new division of butter and margarine. Each person is to get their portion on their own plate. The distribution is very unfair. The van Daans, who always make breakfast for everyone, give themselves one and a half times more than they do us. My parents are much too afraid of an argument to say anything, which is a shame, because I think people like that should always be given a taste of their own medicine.

Yours, Anne

THURSDAY, 4 MARCH 1943

Dearest Kitty,

Mrs van D. has a new nickname – we've started calling her Mrs Beaverbrook. Of course, that doesn't mean anything to you, so let me explain. A certain Mr Beaverbrook often talks on the English radio about what he considers to be the far too lenient bombardment of Germany. Mrs van Daan, who always contradicts everyone, including Churchill and the news reports, is in complete agreement with Mr Beaverbrook. So we thought it would be a good idea for her to be married to him, and since she was flattered by the notion, we've decided to call her Mrs Beaverbrook from now on.

We're getting a new warehouse employee, since the old one is being sent to Germany. That's bad for him but good for us because the new one won't be familiar with the building. We're still afraid of the men who work in the warehouse.

Gandhi is eating again.

The black market is doing a booming business. If we had enough money to pay the ridiculous prices, we could stuff ourselves silly. Our greengrocer buys potatoes from the 'Wehrmacht' and brings them in sacks to the private office.

Since he suspects we're hiding here, he makes a point of coming during lunchtime, when the warehouse employees are out.

So much pepper is being ground at the moment that we sneeze and cough with every breath we take. Everyone who comes upstairs greets us with an 'ah-CHOO'. Mrs van D. swears she won't go downstairs; one more whiff of pepper and she's going to be ill.

I don't think Father has a very nice business. Nothing but pectin and pepper. As long as you're in the food business, why not make sweets?

A veritable thunderstorm of words came crashing down on me again this morning. The air flashed with so many coarse expressions that my ears were ringing with 'Anne's bad this' and 'van Daans' good that'. Fire and brimstone!

Yours, Anne

WEDNESDAY, 10 MARCH 1943

Dearest Kitty,

We had a short circuit last night, and besides that, the guns were booming away until dawn. I still haven't got over my fear of planes and shooting, and I crawl into Father's bed nearly every night for comfort. I know it sounds childish, but wait till it happens to you! The ack-ack guns make so much noise you can't hear your own voice. Mrs Beaverbrook, the fatalist, practically burst into tears and said in a timid little voice, 'Oh, it's so awful. Oh, the guns are so loud!' – which is another way of saying 'I'm so scared'.

It didn't seem nearly as bad by candlelight as it did in the dark. I was shivering, as if I had a temperature, and begged Father to relight the candle. He was adamant: there was to be no light. Suddenly we heard a burst of machine-gun fire, and that's ten times worse than anti-aircraft guns. Mother jumped out of bed and, to Pim's great annoyance, lit the candle. Her resolute answer to his grumbling was, 'After all, Anne is not an ex-soldier!' And that was the end of that!

Have I told you any of Mrs van D.'s other fears? I don't think so. To keep you up to date on the latest adventures in the Secret Annexe, I should tell you this as well. One night Mrs van D. thought she heard loud footsteps in the attic, and she was so afraid of burglars, she woke her husband. At that very same moment, the thieves disappeared, and the only sound Mr van D. could hear was the frightened pounding of his fatalistic wife's heart. 'Oh, Putti!' she cried. (Putti is Mrs van D.'s pet name for her husband.) 'They must have taken all our sausages and dried beans. And what about Peter? Oh, do you think Peter's still safe and sound in his bed?'

'I'm sure they haven't stolen Peter. Stop being such a ninny, and let me get back to sleep!'

Impossible. Mrs van D. was too scared to sleep.

A few nights later the entire van Daan family was awakened by ghostly noises. Peter went to the attic with a torch and – scurry, scurry – what do you think he saw running away? A swarm of enormous rats!

Once we knew who the thieves were, we let Mouschi sleep in the attic and never saw our uninvited guests again . . . at least not at night.

A few evenings ago (it was seven-thirty and still light), Peter went up to the loft to get some old newspapers. He had to hold on tightly to the trapdoor to climb down the ladder. He put down his hand without looking, and nearly fell off the ladder from shock and pain. Without realizing it, he'd put his hand on a large rat, which had bitten him in the arm. By the time he reached us, white as a sheet and with his knees knocking, the blood had soaked through his pyjamas. No wonder he was so shaken – stroking a rat isn't much fun, especially when it takes a chunk out of your arm.

Yours, Anne

Dearest Kitty,

May I introduce: Mother Frank, the children's advocate! Extra butter for the youngsters, the problems facing today's youth – you name it, and she defends the younger generation. After a skirmish or two, she always gets her way.

One of the jars of pickled tongue has gone off. A feast for Mouschi and Boche.

You haven't met Boche yet, despite the fact that she was here before we went into hiding. She's the warehouse and office cat, who keeps the rats at bay in the storeroom. Her odd, political name can easily be explained. For a while the firm of Gies & Co. had two cats: one for the warehouse and one for the attic. Their paths crossed from time to time, which invariably resulted in a fight. The warehouse cat was always the aggressor, while the attic cat was ultimately the victor, just as in politics. So the warehouse cat was named the German, or 'Boche', and the attic cat the Englishman, or 'Tommy'. Some time after that they got rid of Tommy, but Boche is always there to amuse us when we go downstairs.

We've eaten so many brown beans and haricot beans that I can't stand to look at them. Just thinking about them makes me sick.

Our evening serving of bread has been cancelled.

Daddy just said that he's not in a very cheerful mood. His eyes look so sad again, the poor man!

I can't tear myself away from the book *A Knock at the Door* by Ina Bakker Boudier. This family saga is extremely well written, but the parts dealing with war, writers and the emancipation of women aren't very good. To be honest, these subjects don't interest me much.

Terrible bombing raids on Germany. Mr van Daan is grumpy. The reason: the cigarette shortage.

The debate about whether or not to start eating the tinned food ended in our favour.

I can't wear any of my shoes, except my ski boots, which are not very practical around the house. A pair of straw sandals that were purchased for 6.50 guilders were worn down to the soles within a week. Maybe Miep will be able to dig up something on the black market.

It's time to cut Father's hair. Pim swears that I do such a good job he'll never go to another barber after the war. If only I didn't nick his ear so often!

Yours, Anne

THURSDAY, 18 MARCH 1943

My dearest Kitty,

Turkey's entered the war. Great excitement. Anxiously awaiting radio reports.

FRIDAY, 19 MARCH 1943

Dearest Kitty,

In less than an hour, joy was followed by disappointment. Turkey hasn't entered the war yet. It was only a cabinet minister talking about Turkey giving up its neutrality some time soon. The newspaper-seller in Dam Square was shouting 'Turkey on England's side!' and the papers were being snatched out of his hands. This was how we'd heard the encouraging rumour.

Thousand-guilder notes are being declared invalid. That'll be a blow to the black marketeers and others like them, but even more to people in hiding and anyone else with money that can't be accounted for. To turn in a thousand-guilder note, you have to be able to state how you came by it and provide proof. They can still be used to pay taxes, but only until next week. The five-hundred notes will lapse at the same time. Gies & Co. still had some unaccounted-for thousand-guilder notes, which they used to pay their estimated taxes for the coming years, so everything seems to be above board.

Dussel has received an old-fashioned, foot-operated dentist's drill. That means I'll probably be getting a thorough check-up soon.

Dussel is terribly lax when it comes to obeying the rules of the house. Not only does he write letters to his Charlotte, he's also carrying on a chatty correspondence with various other people. Margot, the Annexe's Dutch teacher, has been correcting these letters for him. Father has forbidden him to keep up the practice and Margot has stopped correcting the letters, but I think it won't be long before he starts up again.

The Führer has been talking to wounded soldiers. We heard him on the radio, and it was pathetic. The questions and answers went something like this:

'My name is Heinrich Scheppel.'

'Where were you wounded?'

'Near Stalingrad.'

'What kind of wound is it?'

'Two frostbitten feet and a fracture of the left arm.'

This is an exact report of the hideous puppet show aired on the radio. The wounded seemed proud of their wounds – the more the better. One was so beside himself at the thought of shaking hands (I presume he still had one) with the Führer that he could barely say a word.

I happened to drop Dussel's soap on the floor and step on it. Now there's a whole piece missing. I've already asked Father to compensate him for the damages, especially since Dussel only gets one bar of inferior wartime soap a month.

Yours, Anne

Dearest Kitty,

Mother, Father, Margot and I were sitting quite pleasantly together last night when Peter suddenly came in and whispered in Father's ear. I caught the words 'a barrel falling over in the warehouse' and 'someone fiddling with the door'.

Margot heard it too, but was trying to calm me down, since I'd turned white as chalk and was extremely nervous. The three of us waited while Father and Peter went downstairs. A minute or two later Mrs van Daan came up from where she'd been listening to the radio and told us that Pim had asked her to turn it off and tiptoe upstairs. But you know what happens when you're trying to be quiet – the old stairs creaked twice as loud. Five minutes later Peter and Pim, the colour drained from their faces, appeared again to relate their experiences.

They had positioned themselves under the staircase and waited. Nothing happened. Then all of a sudden they heard a couple of bangs, as if two doors had been slammed shut inside the house. Pim bounded up the stairs, while Peter went to warn Dussel, who finally presented himself upstairs, though not without kicking up a fuss and making a lot of noise. Then we all tiptoed in our stockinged feet to the van Daans on the next floor. Mr van D. had a bad cold and had already gone to bed, so we gathered around his bedside and discussed our suspicions in a whisper. Every time Mr van D. coughed loudly, Mrs van D. and I nearly had a nervous fit. He kept coughing until someone came up with the bright idea of giving him codeine. His cough subsided immediately.

Once again we waited and waited, but heard nothing. Finally we came to the conclusion that the burglars had taken to their heels when they heard footsteps in an otherwise quiet building. The problem now was that the chairs in the private office were neatly grouped around the radio, which was tuned to England. If the burglars had forced the door and the air-raid wardens were to notice it and call the police, there could be very serious repercussions. So Mr van Daan got up, pulled on his coat and trousers, put on his hat and cautiously followed Father down the stairs, with Peter (armed with a heavy hammer, to be on the safe side) right behind him. The ladies (including Margot and me) waited in suspense until the men returned five minutes later and reported that there was no sign of any activity in the building. We agreed not to run any water or flush the toilet; but since everyone's stomach was churning from all the tension, you can imagine the stench after we'd each had a turn in the lavatory.

Incidents like these are always accompanied by other disasters, and this was no exception. Number one: the Westertoren bells stopped chiming, and I'd always found them so comforting. Number two: Mr Voskuijl left early last night, and we weren't sure if he'd given Bep the key and she'd forgotten to lock the door.

But that was of little importance now. The night had just begun, and we still weren't sure what to expect. We were somewhat reassured by the fact that between eight-fifteen –

when the burglar had first entered the building and put our lives in jeopardy – and ten-thirty, we hadn't heard a sound. The more we thought about it, the less likely it seemed that a burglar would have forced a door so early in the evening, when there were still people out on the streets. Besides that, it occurred to us that the warehouse manager at the Keg Company next door might still have been at work. What with the excitement and the thin walls, it's easy to mistake the sounds. Besides, your imagination often plays tricks on you in moments of danger.

So we went to bed, though not to sleep. Father and Mother and Mr Dussel were awake most of the night, and I'm not exaggerating when I say that I hardly got a wink of sleep. This morning the men went downstairs to see if the outside door was still locked, but all was well!

Of course, we gave the entire office staff a blow-by-blow account of the incident, which had been far from pleasant. It's much easier to laugh at these kinds of things after they've happened, and Bep was the only one who took us seriously.

Yours, Anne

PS. This morning the toilet was clogged, and Father had to stick a long wooden pole and fish out several pounds of excrement and strawberry recipes (which is what we use for toilet paper these days). Afterwards we burned the pole.

SATURDAY, 27 MARCH 1943

Dearest Kitty,

We've finished our shorthand course and are now working on improving our speed. Aren't we clever! Let me tell you more about my 'time killers' (this is what I call my courses, because all we ever do is try to make the days go by as quickly as possible so we're that much closer to the end of our time here). I adore mythology, especially the Greek and Roman gods. Everyone here thinks my interest is just a passing fancy, since they've never heard of a teenager with an appreciation of mythology. Well then, I suppose I'm the first!

Mr van Daan has a cold. Or rather, he has a scratchy throat, but he's making an enormous to-do over it. He gargles with camomile tea, coats the roof of his mouth with a tincture of myrrh and rubs Vick on his chest, nose, gums and tongue. And to top it off, he's in a foul mood!

Rauter, some German bigwig, recently gave a speech. 'All Jews must be out of the German-occupied territories before 1 July. The province of Utrecht will be cleansed of Jews [as if they were cockroaches] between 1 April and 1 May, and the provinces of North and South Holland between 1 May and 1 June.' These poor people are being shipped off to filthy slaughterhouses like a herd of sick and neglected cattle. But I'll say no more on the subject. My own thoughts give me nightmares!

One good piece of news is that the Labour Exchange was set on fire in an act of sabotage. A few days later the Register Office also went up in flames. Men posing as German police bound and gagged the guards and managed to destroy some important documents.

Yours, Anne

THURSDAY, 1 APRIL 1943

Dearest Kitty,

I'm not really in the mood for pranks (see the date). On the contrary, today I can safely quote the saying 'Misfortunes never come singly'.

First, Mr Kleiman, our merry ray of sunshine, had another bout of gastro-intestinal haemorrhaging yesterday and will have to stay in bed for at least three weeks. I should tell you that his stomach has been bothering him quite a bit, and there's no cure. Second, Bep has flu. Third, Mr Voskuijl has to go into hospital next week. He probably has an ulcer and will have to undergo surgery. Fourth, the managers of Pomosin Industries came from Frankfurt to discuss the new Opekta deliveries. Father had gone over the important points with Mr Kleiman, and there wasn't enough time to give Mr Kugler a thorough briefing.

The gentlemen arrived from Frankfurt, and Father was already shaking at the thought of how the talks would go. 'If only I could be there, if only I were downstairs,' he exclaimed.

'Go and lie down with your ear to the floor. They'll be brought to the private office, and you'll be able to hear everything.'

Father's face cleared, and yesterday morning at ten-thirty Margot and Pim (two ears are better than one) took up their posts on the floor. By noon the talks weren't finished, but Father was in no shape to continue his listening campaign. He was in agony from having to lie for hours in such an unusual and uncomfortable position. At two-thirty we heard voices in the passage, and I took his place; Margot kept me company. The conversation was so long-winded and boring that I suddenly fell asleep on the cold, hard linoleum. Margot didn't dare touch me for fear they'd hear us, and of course she couldn't shout. I slept for a good half-hour and then awoke with a start, having forgotten every word of the important discussion. Luckily, Margot had paid more attention.

Yours, Anne

Dearest Kitty,

Oh my, another item has been added to my list of sins. Last night I was lying in bed, waiting for Father to tuck me in and say my prayers with me, when Mother came into the room, sat on my bed and asked very gently, 'Anne, Daddy isn't ready. What if I listen to your prayers tonight?'

'No, Mumsie,' I replied.

Mother got up, stood beside my bed for a moment and then slowly walked towards the door. Suddenly she turned, her face contorted with pain, and said, 'I don't want to be angry with you. I can't make you love me!' A few tears slid down her cheeks as she went out of the door.

I lay still, thinking how mean it was of me to reject her so cruelly, but I also knew that I was incapable of answering her any other way. I can't be a hypocrite and pray with her when I don't feel like it. It just doesn't work that way. I felt sorry for Mother – very, very sorry – because for the first time in my life I noticed she wasn't indifferent to my coldness. I saw the sorrow in her face when she talked about not being able to make me love her. It's hard to tell the truth, and yet the truth is that she's the one who's rejected me. She's the one whose tactless comments and cruel jokes about matters I don't think are funny have made me insensitive to any sign of love on her part. Just as my heart sinks every time I hear her harsh words, that's how her heart sank when she realized there was no more love between us.

She cried half the night and didn't get any sleep. Father has avoided looking at me, and if his eyes do happen to meet mine, I can read his unspoken words: 'How can you be so unkind? How dare you make your mother so sad!'

Everyone expects me to apologize, but this is not something

99

I can apologize for, because I told the truth, and sooner or later Mother was bound to find out anyway. I seem to be indifferent to Mother's tears and Father's glances, and I am, because both of them are now feeling what I've always felt. I can only feel sorry for Mother, who will have to decide what her attitude should be all by herself. For my part, I will continue to remain silent and aloof, and I don't intend to shrink from the truth, because the longer it's postponed, the harder it will be for them to accept it when they do hear it!

Yours, Anne

TUESDAY, 27 APRIL 1943

Dearest Kitty,

The house is still trembling from the after-effects of the quarrels. Everyone is angry with everyone else: Mother and I, Mr van Daan and Father, Mother and Mrs van D. Terrific atmosphere, don't you think? Once again Anne's usual list of shortcomings has been extensively aired.

Our German visitors were back last Saturday. They stayed until six. We all sat upstairs, not daring to move an inch. If there's no one else working in the building or in the neighbourhood, you can hear every single step in the private office. I've got ants in my pants again from having to sit still so long.

Mr Voskuijl has been hospitalized, but Mr Kleiman's back at the office. His stomach stopped bleeding sooner than it normally does. He told us that the Register Office took an extra beating because the firemen flooded the entire building instead of just putting out the fire. That does my heart good!

The Carlton Hotel has been destroyed. Two British planes loaded with firebombs landed right on top of the German Officers' Club. The entire corner of Vijzelstraat and Singel has gone up in flames. The number of air strikes on German cities is increasing daily. We haven't had a good night's rest in ages, and I have bags under my eyes from lack of sleep.

Our food is terrible. Breakfast consists of plain, unbuttered bread and ersatz coffee. For the last two weeks lunch has been either spinach or cooked lettuce with huge potatoes that have a rotten, sweetish taste. If you're trying to slim, the Annexe is the place to be! Upstairs they complain bitterly, but we don't think it's such a tragedy.

All the Dutch men who either fought or were mobilized in 1940 have been called up to work in prisoner-of-war camps. I bet they're taking this precaution because of the invasion!

Yours, Anne

SATURDAY, 1 MAY 1943

Dearest Kitty,

Yesterday was Dussel's birthday. At first he acted as if he didn't want to celebrate it, but when Miep arrived with a large shopping bag overflowing with gifts, he was as excited as a little child. His darling 'Lotje' has sent him eggs, butter, biscuits, lemonade, bread, cognac, spice cake, flowers, oranges, chocolate, books and writing paper. He piled his presents on a table and displayed them for no fewer than three days, the ridiculous old fool!

You mustn't get the idea that he's starving. We found bread, cheese, jam and eggs in his cupboard. It's absolutely disgraceful that Dussel, whom we've treated with such kindness and whom we took in to save from destruction, should stuff himself behind our backs and not give us anything. After all, we've shared all we had with him! But what's worse, in our opinion, is that he's so stingy with respect to Mr Kleiman, Mr Voskuijl and Bep. He doesn't give them a thing. In Dussel's view the oranges that Kleiman so badly needs for his sick stomach will benefit his own stomach even more.

Tonight the guns have been banging away so much that I've already had to gather up my belongings four times. Today I packed a suitcase with the stuff I'd need in case we had to flee, but as Mother correctly noted, 'Where would you go?'

All of Holland is being punished for the workers' strikes. Martial law has been declared, and everyone is going to get one less butter coupon. What naughty children.

I washed Mother's hair this evening, which is no easy task these days. We have to use a very sticky liquid cleanser because there's no more shampoo. Besides that, Mums had a hard time combing her hair because the family comb has only ten teeth left.

Yours, Anne

SUNDAY, 2 MAY 1943

When I think about our lives here, I usually come to the conclusion that we live in a paradise compared with the Jews who aren't in hiding. All the same, later on, when everything has returned to normal, I'll probably wonder how we, who always lived in such comfortable circumstances, could have 'sunk' so low. With respect to manners, I mean. For example, the same oilcloth has covered the dining-table ever since we've been here. After so much use, it's hardly what you'd call spotless. I do my best to clean it, but since the dishcloth was also purchased before we went into hiding and consists of more holes than cloth, it's a thankless task. The van Daans have been sleeping all winter long on the same flannelette sheet, which can't be washed because soap powder is rationed and in short supply. Besides, it's of such poor quality that it's practically useless. Father is walking around in frayed trousers, and his tie is also showing signs of wear and tear. Mummy's corset snapped today and is beyond repair, while Margot is wearing a bra that's two sizes too small. Mother and Margot have shared the same three vests the entire winter, and mine are so small they don't even cover my stomach. These are all things that can be overcome, but I sometimes wonder: how can we, whose every possession, from my knickers to Father's shaving brush, is so old and worn, ever hope to regain the position we had before the war?

SUNDAY, 2 MAY 1943

The Attitude of the Annexe Residents Towards the War

Mr van Daan. In the opinion of us all, this revered gentleman has great insight into politics. Nevertheless, he predicts we'll have to stay here until the end of '43. That's a very long time, and yet it's possible to hold out until then. But who can assure us that this war, which has caused nothing but pain and sorrow, will then be over? And that nothing will have happened to us and our helpers long before that time? No one! That's why each and every day is filled with tension. Expectation and hope generate tension, as does fear – for example, when we hear a noise inside or outside the house, when the guns go off or when we read new 'proclamations' in the paper, since we're afraid our helpers might be forced to go into hiding themselves sometime. These days everyone is talking about having to hide. We don't know how many people are actually in hiding; of course, the number is relatively small compared with the general population, but later on we'll no doubt be astonished at how many good people in Holland were willing to take Jews and Christians, with or without money, into their homes. There're also an unbelievable number of people with false identity papers.

Mrs van Daan. When this beautiful damsel (by her own account) heard that it was getting easier these days to obtain false IDs, she immediately proposed that we each have one made. As if there were nothing to it, as if Father and Mr van Daan were made of money.

Mrs van Daan is always saying the most ridiculous things, and her Putti is often exasperated. But that's not surprising, because one day Kerli announces, 'When this is all over, I'm going to have myself baptized'; and the next, 'As long as I can remember, I've wanted to go to Jerusalem. I only feel at home with other Jews!'

Pim is a big optimist, but he always has his reasons.

Mr Dussel makes up everything as he goes along, and anyone wishing to contradict His Majesty had better think twice. In Albert Dussel's home his word is law, but that doesn't suit Anne Frank in the least.

What the other members of the Annexe family think about the war doesn't matter. When it comes to politics, these four are the only ones who count. Actually, only two of them do, but Madame van Daan and Dussel include themselves as well.

TUESDAY, 18 MAY 1943

Dearest Kit,

I recently witnessed a fierce dogfight between German and English pilots. Unfortunately, a couple of Allied airmen had to jump out of their burning plane. Our milkman, who lives in Halfweg, saw four Canadians sitting along the side of the road, and one of them spoke fluent Dutch. He asked the milkman if he had a light for his cigarette, and then told him the crew had consisted of six men. The pilot had been burned to death, and the fifth crew member had hidden himself somewhere. The German Security Police came to pick up the four remaining men, none of whom was injured. After parachuting out of a flaming plane, how can anyone have such presence of mind?

Although it's undeniably hot, we have to light a fire every other day to burn our vegetable peelings and rubbish. We can't throw anything into the dustbins, because the warehouse employees might see it. One small act of carelessness and we're done for!

All university students are being asked to sign an official statement to the effect that they 'sympathize with the Germans and approve of the New Order'. Eighty per cent have decided to obey the dictates of their conscience, but the penalty will be severe. Any student refusing to sign will be sent to a German labour camp. What's to become of the youth of our country if they've all got to do hard labour in Germany?

Last night the guns were making so much noise that Mother shut the window; I was in Pim's bed. Suddenly, right above our heads, we heard Mrs van D. leap up, as if she'd been bitten by Mouschi. This was followed by a loud boom, which sounded as if a firebomb had landed beside my bed. 'Lights! Lights!' I screamed.

Pim switched on the lamp. I expected the room to burst into flames any minute. Nothing happened. We all rushed upstairs to see what was going on. Mr and Mrs van D. had seen a red glow through the open window, and he thought there was a fire nearby, while she was certain our house was ablaze. Mrs van D. was already standing beside her bed with her knees knocking when the boom came. Dussel stayed upstairs to smoke a cigarette, and we crawled back into bed. Less than fifteen minutes later the shooting started again. Mrs van D. sprang out of bed and went downstairs to Dussel's room to seek the comfort she was unable to find with her spouse. Dussel welcomed her with the words 'Come into my bed, my child!'

We burst into peals of laughter, and the roar of the guns bothered us no more; our fears had all been swept away.

Yours, Anne

SUNDAY, 13 JUNE 1943

Dearest Kitty,

The poem Father composed for my birthday is too nice to keep to myself.

Since Pim writes his verses only in German, Margot volunteered to translate it into Dutch. See for yourself whether Margot hasn't done herself proud. It begins with the usual summary of the year's events and then continues:

> *As youngest among us, but small no more,*
> *Your life can be trying, for we have the chore*
> *Of becoming your teachers, a terrible bore.*
> *'We've got experience! Take it from me!'*
> *'We've done this all before, you see.*
> *We know the ropes, we know the game.'*
> *Since time immemorial, always the same.*
> *One's own shortcomings are nothing but fluff,*
> *But everyone else's are heavier stuff.*
> *Fault-finding comes easy when this is our plight,*
> *But it's hard for your parents, try as they might,*
> *To treat you with fairness, and kindness as well;*

Nit-picking's a habit that's hard to dispel.
When you're living with old folk, all you can do
Is put up with their nagging – it's hard but it's true.
The pill may be bitter, but down it must go,
For it's meant to keep the peace, you know.
The many months here have not been in vain,
Since wasting time goes against your grain.
You read and study nearly all the day,
Determined to chase the boredom away.
The more difficult question, much harder to bear,
Is 'What on earth do I have to wear?
I've got no more knickers, my clothes are too tight,
My vest is a loincloth, I'm really a sight!
To put on my shoes I must cut off my toes,
Oh dear, I'm plagued with so many woes!'

Margot had trouble getting the part about food to rhyme, so I'm leaving it out. But aside from that, don't you think it's a good poem?

For the rest, I've been thoroughly spoiled and have received a number of lovely presents, including a big book on my favourite subject, Greek and Roman mythology. Nor can I complain about the lack of sweets; everyone had dipped into their last reserves. As the Benjamin of the Annexe, I got more than I deserve.

Yours, Anne

TUESDAY, 15 JUNE 1943

Dearest Kitty,

Heaps of things have happened, but I often think I'm boring you with my dreary chitchat and that you'd just as soon have fewer letters. So I'll keep the news brief.

Mr Voskuijl wasn't operated on for his ulcer after all. Once the doctors had him on the operating table and opened him up, they saw that he had cancer. It was in such an advanced stage that an operation was pointless. So they stitched him up again, kept him in hospital for three weeks, fed him well and sent him back home. But they made an unforgivable error: they told the poor man exactly what was in store for him. He can't work any more, and he's just sitting at home, surrounded by his eight children, brooding about his approaching death. I feel very sorry for him and hate not being able to go out; otherwise, I'd visit him as often as I could and help take his mind off matters. Now the good man can no longer let us know what's being said and done in the warehouse, which is a disaster for us. Mr Voskuijl was our greatest source of help and support when it came to safety measures. We miss him very much.

Next month it's our turn to hand over our radio to the authorities. Mr Kleiman has a small set hidden in his home that he's giving us to replace our beautiful Philips. It's a pity we have to turn in our big one, but when you're in hiding, you can't afford to bring the authorities down on your heads. Of course, we'll put the 'baby' radio upstairs. What's a clandestine radio when there are already clandestine Jews and clandestine money?

All over the country people are trying to get hold of an old radio that they can hand over instead of their 'morale booster'. It's true: as the reports from outside grow worse and worse, the radio, with its wondrous voice, helps us not to lose heart and to keep telling ourselves, 'Cheer up, keep your spirits high, things are bound to get better!'

Yours, Anne

Dear Kitty,

To get back to the subject of child-rearing (for the umpteenth time), let me tell you that I'm doing my best to be helpful, friendly and kind and to do all I can to keep the rain of rebukes down to a light drizzle. It's not easy trying to behave like a model child with people you can't stand, especially when you don't mean a word of it. But I can see that a little hypocrisy gets me a lot further than my old method of saying exactly what I think (even though no one ever asks my opinion or cares one way or another). Of course, I often forget my role and find it impossible to curb my anger when they're unfair, so that they spend the next month saying I'm the cheekiest girl in the world. Don't you think I'm to be pitied sometimes? It's a good thing I'm not a moaner, because then I might become sour and bad-tempered. I can usually see the humorous side of their scoldings, but it's easier when somebody else is being hauled over the coals.

Further, I've decided (after a great deal of thought) to drop the shorthand. First, so that I have more time for my other subjects, and second, because of my eyes. That's a sad story. I've become very short-sighted and should have had glasses ages ago. (Ugh, won't I look like a muggins!) But as you know, people in hiding can't . . .

Yesterday all anyone here could talk about was Anne's eyes, because Mother had suggested I go to the specialist with Mrs Kleiman. Just hearing this made my knees weak, since it's no small matter. Going outside! Just think of it, walking down the *street*! I can't imagine it. I was petrified at first, and then glad. But it's not as simple as all that; the various authorities who had to approve such a step were unable to reach a quick decision. They first had to carefully weigh all the difficulties and risks, though Miep was ready to set off immediately with me in tow. In the meantime, I'd taken my grey coat from the wardrobe, but it was so small it looked as if it might have belonged to my little sister. We lowered the hem, but I still couldn't button it. I'm really curious to see what they decide, only I don't think they'll ever work out a plan, because the British have landed in Sicily and Father's all set for a 'quick finish'.

Bep's been giving Margot and me a lot of office work to do. It makes us both feel important, and it's a big help to her. Anyone can file letters and make entries in a sales book, but we do it with remarkable accuracy.

Miep has so much to carry she looks like a pack mule. She goes out nearly every day in search of vegetables, and then cycles back with her purchases in large shopping bags. She's also the one who brings five library books with her every Saturday. We long for Saturdays because that means books. We're like a lot of little children with a present. Ordinary people don't know how much books can mean to someone who's cooped up. Our only diversions are reading, studying and listening to the wireless.

Yours, Anne

TUESDAY, 13 JULY 1943

The Best Little Table

Yesterday afternoon Father gave me permission to ask Mr Dussel whether he would please be so good as to allow me (see how polite I am?) to use the table in our room two afternoons a week, from four to five-thirty. I already sit there every day from two-thirty to four while Dussel has a nap, but the rest of the time the room and the table are out of bounds to me. It's impossible to study next door in the afternoon, because there's too much going on. Besides, Father sometimes likes to sit at the desk during the afternoon.

So it seemed like a reasonable request, and I asked Dussel very politely. What do you think the learned gentleman's reply was? 'No.' Just plain 'No'!

I was incensed and wasn't about to let myself be put off like that. I asked him the reason for his 'No', but this didn't get me anywhere. The gist of his reply was: 'I have to study too, you know, and if I can't do that in the afternoons, I won't be able to fit it in at all. I have to finish the task I've set for myself; otherwise, there's no point in starting. Besides, you aren't serious about your studies. Mythology – what kind of work is that? Reading and knitting don't count either. I use that table and I'm not going to give it up!'

I replied, 'Mr Dussel, I do take my work seriously. I can't study next door in the afternoons, and I would appreciate it if you would reconsider my request!'

Having said these words, the insulted Anne turned round and pretended the learned doctor wasn't there. I was seething with rage and felt that Dussel had been incredibly rude (which he certainly had been) and that I'd been very polite.

That evening, when I managed to get hold of Pim, I told him what had happened and we discussed what my next step should be, because I had no intention of giving up and preferred to deal with the matter myself. Pim gave me a rough idea of how to approach Dussel, but cautioned me to wait until the next day, since I was in such a flap. I ignored this last piece of advice and waited for Dussel after I'd done the washing-up. Pim was sitting next door and that had a calming effect.

I began, 'Mr Dussel, you seem to believe further discussion

of the matter is pointless, but I beg you to reconsider.'

Dussel gave me his most charming smile and said, 'I'm always prepared to discuss the matter, even though it's already been settled.'

I went on talking, despite Dussel's repeated interruptions. 'When you first came here,' I said, 'we agreed that the room was to be shared by the two of us. If we were to divide it fairly, you'd have the entire morning and I'd have the entire afternoon! I'm not asking for that much, but two afternoons a week does seem reasonable to me.'

Dussel leapt out of his chair as if he'd sat on a pin. 'You have no business talking about your rights to the room. Where am I supposed to go? Maybe I should ask Mr van Daan to build me a cubbyhole in the attic. You're not the only one who can't find a quiet place to work. You're always looking for a fight. If your sister Margot, who has more right to work space than you do, had come to me with the same request, I'd never even have thought of refusing, but you . . .'

And once again he brought up the business about the mythology and the knitting, and once again Anne was insulted. However, I showed no sign of it and let Dussel finish: 'But no, it's impossible to talk to you. You're shamefully self-centred. No one else matters, as long as you get your way. I've never seen such a child. But after all is said and done, I'll be obliged to let you have your way, since I don't want people saying later on that Anne Frank failed her exams because Mr Dussel refused to relinquish his table!'

He went on and on until there was such a deluge of words I could hardly keep up. For one fleeting moment I thought, 'Him and his lies. I'll smack his ugly mug so hard he'll go bouncing off the wall!' But the next moment I thought, 'Calm down, he's not worth getting so upset about!'

At long last Mr Dussel's fury was spent, and he left the

room with an expression of triumph mixed with wrath, his coat pockets bulging with food.

I went running over to Father and recounted the entire story, or at least those parts he hadn't been able to follow himself. Pim decided to talk to Dussel that very same evening, and they spoke for more than half an hour. They first discussed whether Anne should be allowed to use the table, yes or no. Father said that he and Dussel had dealt with the subject once before, at which time he'd professed to agree with Dussel because he didn't want to contradict the elder in front of the younger, but that, even then, he hadn't thought it was fair. Dussel felt I had no right to talk as if he were an intruder laying claim to everything in sight. But Father protested strongly, since he himself had heard me say nothing of the kind. And so the conversation went back and forth, with Father defending my 'selfishness' and my 'pointless activities' and Dussel grumbling the whole time.

Dussel finally had to give in, and I was granted the opportunity to work without interruption two afternoons a week. Dussel looked very sullen, didn't speak to me for two days and made sure he occupied the table from five to five-thirty – all very childish, of course.

Anyone who's so petty and pedantic at the age of fifty-four was born that way and is never going to change.

FRIDAY, 16 JULY 1943

Dearest Kitty,

There's been another break-in, but this time a real one! Peter went down to the warehouse this morning at seven, as usual, and noticed at once that both the warehouse door and the street door were open. He immediately reported this to Pim, who went to the private office, tuned the radio to a

German station and locked the door. Then they both went back upstairs. In such cases our orders are 'not to wash ourselves or run any water, to be quiet, to be dressed by eight and not to go to the lavatory', and as usual we followed these to the letter. We were all glad we'd slept so well and hadn't heard anything. For a while we were indignant because no one from the office came upstairs the entire morning; Mr Kleiman left us on tenterhooks until eleven-thirty. He told us that the burglars had forced the outside door and the warehouse door with a crowbar, but when they didn't find anything worth stealing, they tried their luck on the next floor. They stole two cash-boxes containing 40 guilders, blank chequebooks and, worst of all, coupons for 330 pounds of sugar, our entire allotment. It won't be easy to wangle new ones.

Mr Kugler thinks this burglar belongs to the same gang as the one who made an unsuccessful attempt six weeks ago to open all three doors (the warehouse door and the two outside doors).

The burglary caused another stir, but the Annexe seems to thrive on excitement. Naturally, we were glad the cash register and the typewriters had been safely tucked away in our wardrobe.

Yours, Anne

PS. Landing in Sicily. Another step closer to the . . . !

MONDAY, 19 JULY 1943

Dearest Kitty,

North Amsterdam was very heavily bombed on Sunday. There was apparently a great deal of destruction. Entire streets are in ruins, and it will take a while for them to dig out all the bodies. So far there have been two hundred dead and countless wounded; the hospitals are bursting at the seams. We've been told of children searching forlornly in the smouldering ruins for their dead parents. It still makes me shiver to think of the dull, distant drone that signified the approaching destruction.

Bep is currently able to get hold of exercise-books, especially journals and ledgers, useful for my bookkeeping sister! Other kinds are for sale as well, but don't ask what they're like or how long they'll last. At the moment they're all labelled 'No Coupons Needed'! Like everything else you can purchase without ration stamps, they're totally worthless. They consist of twelve sheets of grey paper with narrow lines that slant across the page. Margot is thinking about taking a course in calligraphy; I've advised her to go ahead and do it. Mother won't let me because of my eyes, but I think that's silly. Whether I do that or something else, it all comes down to the same thing.

Since you've never been through a war, Kitty, and since you know very little about life in hiding, in spite of my letters, let me tell you, just for fun, what we each want to do first when we're able to go outside again.

Margot and Mr van Daan wish, above all else, to have a hot bath, filled to the brim, which they can lie in for more than half an hour. Mrs van Daan would like a cake, Dussel can think of nothing but seeing his Charlotte, and Mother is dying for a cup of real coffee. Father would like to visit Mr Voskuijl, Peter would go into town, and as for me, I'd be so overjoyed I wouldn't know where to begin.

Most of all I long to have a home of our own, to be able to move around freely and have someone help me with my homework again, at last. In other words, to go back to school!

Bep has offered to get us some fruit, at so-called bargain prices: grapes 2.50 guilders a pound, gooseberries 70 cents a pound, one peach 50 cents, melons 75 cents a pound. No wonder the papers write every evening in big, fat letters: 'Play Fair and Keep Prices Down'!

MONDAY, 26 JULY 1943

Dear Kitty,

Yesterday was a very tumultuous day, and we're still all wound up. Actually, you may wonder if there's ever a day that passes without some kind of excitement.

The first warning siren went off in the morning while we were at breakfast, but we paid no attention, because it only meant that the planes were crossing the coast. I had a terrible headache, so I lay down for an hour after breakfast and then went to the office at about two. At two-thirty Margot had finished her office work and was just gathering her things together when the sirens began wailing again. So she and I trooped back upstairs. None too soon, it seems, for less than five minutes later the guns were booming so loudly that we went and stood in the passage. The house shook and the bombs kept falling. I was clutching my 'escape bag', more because I wanted to have something to hold on to than because I wanted to run away. I know we can't leave here, but if we had to, being seen on the streets would be just as dangerous as getting caught in an air raid. After half an hour the drone of engines faded and the house began to hum with activity again. Peter emerged from his lookout post in the front attic, Dussel remained in the front office, Mrs van D. felt safest in the private office, Mr van Daan had been watching from the loft, and those of us on the landing spread out to watch the columns of smoke rising from the harbour. Before long the smell of fire was everywhere, and outside it looked as if the city were enveloped in a thick fog.

A big fire like that is not a pleasant sight, but fortunately for us it was all over, and we went back to our various jobs. Just as we were starting dinner: another air-raid alarm. The food was good, but I lost my appetite the moment I heard the siren. Nothing happened, however, and forty-five minutes later the all-clear was sounded. After the washing-up: another air-raid warning, gunfire and swarms of planes. 'Oh, gosh, twice in one day,' we thought, 'that's twice too many.' Little good that did us, because once again the bombs rained down, this time on the other side of the city. According to British reports, Schiphol Airport was bombed. The planes dived and climbed, the air was abuzz with the drone of engines. It was very scary, and the whole time I kept thinking, 'Here it comes, this is it.'

I can assure you that when I went to bed at nine, my legs were still shaking. At the stroke of midnight I woke up again: more planes! Dussel was undressing, but I took no notice and leapt up, wide awake, at the sound of the first shot. I stayed in Father's bed until one, in my own bed until one-thirty, and was back in Father's bed at two. But the planes kept on coming. At last they stopped firing and I was able to go back 'home' again. I finally fell asleep at half past two.

Seven o'clock. I awoke with a start and sat up in bed. Mr van Daan was with Father. My first thought was: burglars. 'Everything,' I heard Mr van Daan say, and I thought everything had been stolen. But no, this time it was wonderful news, the best we've had in months, maybe even since the war began. Mussolini has resigned and the King of Italy has taken over the government.

We jumped for joy. After the awful events of yesterday, finally something good happens and brings us . . . hope! Hope for an end to the war, hope for peace.

Mr Kugler popped in and told us that the Fokker aircraft factory had been hit hard. Meanwhile, there was another air-raid alarm this morning, with planes flying over, and another warning siren. I've had it up to here with alarms. I've hardly slept, and the last thing I want to do is work. But now the suspense about Italy and the hope that the war will be over by the end of the year are keeping us awake . . .

Yours, Anne

THURSDAY, 29 JULY 1943

Dearest Kitty,

Mrs van Daan, Dussel and I were doing the washing-up, and I was extremely quiet. This is very unusual for me and they were sure to notice, so in order to avoid any questions, I quickly racked my brains for a neutral topic. I thought the book *Henry from Across the Street* might fit the bill, but I couldn't have been more wrong; if Mrs van Daan doesn't jump down my throat, Mr Dussel does. It all boiled down to this: Mr Dussel had recommended the book to Margot and me as an example of excellent writing. We thought it was anything but that. The little boy had been portrayed well, but as for the rest . . . the less said the better. I mentioned something to that effect while we were washing up, and Dussel launched into a veritable tirade.

'How can you possibly understand the psychology of a man? That of a child isn't so difficult [!]. But you're far too young to read a book like that. Even a twenty-year-old man would be unable to comprehend it.' (So why did he go out of his way to recommend it to Margot and me?)

Mrs van D. and Dussel continued their harangue: 'You know far too much about things you're not supposed to. You've been brought up all wrong. Later on, when you're older, you won't be able to enjoy anything any more. You'll say, "Oh, I read that twenty years ago in some book." You'd better hurry if you want to catch a husband or fall in love, since everything is bound to be a disappointment to you. You already know all there is to know in theory. But in practice? That's another story!'

Can you imagine how I felt? I astonished myself by calmly replying, 'You may think I haven't been raised properly, but many people would disagree!'

They apparently believe that good child-rearing includes trying to pit me against my parents, since that's all they ever do. And not telling a girl my age about grown-up subjects is fine. We can all see what happens when people are raised that way.

At that moment I could have slapped them both for poking fun at me. I was beside myself with rage, and if I only knew how much longer we had to put up with each other's company, I'd start counting the days.

Mrs van Daan's a fine one to talk! She sets an example all right – a bad one! She's known to be exceedingly pushy, egotistical, cunning, calculating and perpetually dissatisfied. Add to that, vanity and coquettishness and there's no question about it: she's a thoroughly despicable person. I could write an entire book about Madame van Daan, and who knows, maybe someday I will. Anyone can put on a charming exterior when they want to. Mrs van D. is friendly to strangers, especially men, so it's easy to make a mistake when you first get to know her.

Mother thinks that Mrs van D. is too stupid for words, Margot that she's too unimportant, Pim that she's too ugly (literally and figuratively!), and after long observation (I'm never prejudiced at the beginning), I've come to the conclusion that she's all three of the above, and lots more besides. She has so many bad traits, why should I single out just one of them?

Yours, Anne

PS. Will the reader please take into consideration that this story was written before the writer's fury had cooled?

TUESDAY, 3 AUGUST 1943

Dearest Kitty,

Things are going well on the political front. Italy has banned the Fascist Party. The people are fighting the Fascists in many places – even the army has joined the fight. How can a country like that continue to wage war against England?

Our beautiful radio was taken away last week. Dussel was very angry at Mr Kugler for turning it in on the appointed day. Dussel is slipping lower and lower in my estimation, and he's already below zero. Whatever he says about politics, history, geography or anything else is so ridiculous that I hardly dare repeat it: Hitler will fade from history; the harbour in Rotterdam is bigger than the one in Hamburg; the English are idiots for not taking the opportunity to bomb Italy to smithereens; etc., etc.

We just had a third air raid. I decided to grit my teeth and practise being courageous.

Mrs van Daan, the one who always said 'Let them fall' and 'Better to end with a bang than not to end at all', is the most cowardly one among us. She was shaking like a leaf this morning and even burst into tears. She was comforted by her husband, with whom she recently declared a truce after a week of squabbling; I nearly got sentimental at the sight.

Mouschi has now proved, beyond a shadow of a doubt, that having a cat has disadvantages as well as advantages. The whole house is crawling with fleas, and it's getting worse each day. Mr Kleiman sprinkled yellow powder in every nook and cranny, but the fleas haven't taken the slightest notice. It's making us all very jittery; we're forever imagining a bite on our arms and legs or other parts of our bodies, so we leap up and do a few exercises, since it gives us an excuse to take a better look at our arms or necks. But now we're paying the price for having had so little physical exercise; we're so stiff we can hardly turn our heads. The real calisthenics fell by the wayside long ago.

Yours, Anne

WEDNESDAY, 4 AUGUST 1943

Dearest Kitty,

Now that we've been in hiding for a little over a year, you know a great deal about our lives. Still, I can't possibly tell you everything, since it's all so different compared with ordinary times and ordinary people. Nevertheless, to give you a closer look into our lives, from time to time I'll describe part of an ordinary day. I'll start with the evening and night.

Nine in the evening. Bedtime always begins in the Annexe with an enormous hustle and bustle. Chairs are shifted, beds pulled out, blankets unfolded – nothing stays where it is during the daytime. I sleep on a small divan, which is only five feet long, so we have to add a few chairs to make it longer. Eiderdown, sheets, pillows, blankets: everything has to be removed from Dussel's bed, where it's kept during the day.

In the next room there's a terrible creaking: that's Margot's folding bed being set up. More blankets and pillows, anything to make the wooden slats a bit more comfortable. Upstairs it sounds like thunder, but it's only Mrs van D.'s bed being shoved against the window so that Her Majesty, arrayed in her pink bed jacket, can sniff the night air through her delicate little nostrils.

Nine o'clock. After Peter's finished, it's my turn for the bathroom. I wash myself from head to toe, and more often than not I find a tiny flea floating in the sink (only during the hot months, weeks or days). I brush my teeth, curl my hair, manicure my nails and dab peroxide on my upper lip to bleach the black hairs – all this in less than half an hour.

Nine-thirty. I throw on my dressing-gown. With soap in one hand, and potty, hairpins, knickers, curlers and cotton wool in the other, I hurry out of the bathroom. The next person in invariably calls me back to remove the gracefully curved but unsightly hairs that I've left in the sink.

Ten o'clock. Time to put up the black-out screen and say good night. For the next fifteen minutes, at least, the house is filled with the creaking of beds and the sigh of broken springs, and then, provided our upstairs neighbours aren't having a marital tiff in bed, all is quiet.

Eleven-thirty. The bathroom door creaks. A narrow strip of light falls into the room. Squeaking shoes, a large coat, even larger than the man inside it . . . Dussel is returning from his nightly work in Mr Kugler's office. I hear him shuffling back and forth for ten whole minutes, the rustle of paper (from the food he's tucking away in his cupboard) and the bed being made up. Then the figure disappears again, and the only sound is the occasional suspicious noise from the lavatory.

Approximately three o'clock. I have to get up to use the tin under my bed, which, to be on the safe side, has a rubber mat underneath in case of leaks. I always hold my breath while I go, since it clatters into the tin like a brook down a mountainside. The potty is returned to its place, and the figure in the white nightdress (the one that causes Margot to exclaim every evening, 'Oh, that indecent nightie!') climbs back into bed. A certain somebody lies awake for about fifteen minutes, listening to the sounds of the night. In the first place, to hear whether there are any burglars downstairs, and then to the various beds – upstairs, next door and in my room – to tell whether the others are asleep or half awake. This is no fun, especially when it concerns a member of the family named Dr Dussel. First, there's the sound of a fish gasping for air, and this is repeated nine or ten times. Then, the lips are moistened profusely. This is alternated with little smacking sounds, followed by a long period of tossing and turning and rearranging the pillows. After five minutes of perfect quiet, the same sequence repeats itself three more times, after which he's presumably lulled himself back to sleep for a while.

Sometimes the guns go off during the night, between one and four. I'm never aware of it before it happens, but all of a sudden I find myself standing beside my bed, out of sheer habit. Occasionally I'm dreaming so deeply (of irregular French verbs or a quarrel upstairs) that I realize only when my dream is over that the shooting has stopped and that I've remained quietly in my room. But usually I wake up. Then I grab a pillow and a handkerchief, throw on my dressing-gown and slippers and dash next door to

Father, just the way Margot described in this birthday poem:

> *When shots ring out in the dark of night,*
> *The door creaks open and into sight*
> *Come a hanky, a pillow, a figure in white . . .*

Once I've reached the big bed, the worst is over, except when the shooting is extra loud.

Six forty-five. Brrring . . . the alarm clock, which raises its shrill voice at any hour of the day or night, whether you want it to or not. Creak . . . wham . . . Mrs van D. turns it off. Screak . . . Mr van D. gets up, puts on the water and races to the bathroom.

Seven-fifteen. The door creaks again. Dussel can go to the bathroom. Alone at last, I remove the black-out screen . . . and a new day begins in the Annexe.

Yours, Anne

THURSDAY, 5 AUGUST 1943

Dearest Kitty,

Today let's talk about the lunch break.

It's twelve-thirty. The whole gang breathes a sigh of relief: Mr van Maaren, the man with the shady past, and Mr de Kok have gone home for lunch.

Upstairs you can hear the thud of the vacuum cleaner on Mrs van D.'s beautiful and only rug. Margot tucks a few books under her arm and heads for the class for 'slow learners', which is what Dussel seems to be. Pim goes and sits in a corner with his constant companion, Dickens, in hopes of finding a bit of peace and quiet. Mother hastens upstairs to help the busy little housewife, and I tidy up both the bathroom and myself at the same time.

Twelve forty-five. One by one they trickle in: first Mr Gies and then either Mr Kleiman or Mr Kugler, followed by Bep and sometimes even Miep.

One. Clustered round the radio, they all listen raptly to the BBC. This is the only time the members of the Annexe family don't interrupt each other, since even Mr van Daan can't argue with the speaker.

One-fifteen. Food distribution. Everyone from downstairs gets a cup of soup, plus pudding, if there happens to be any. A contented Mr Gies sits on the divan or leans against the desk with his newspaper, cup and usually the cat at his side. If one of the three is missing, he doesn't hesitate to let his protest be heard. Mr Kleiman relates the latest news from town, and he's an excellent source. Mr Kugler hurries up the stairs, gives a short but solid knock on the door and comes in either wringing his hands or rubbing them in glee, depending on whether he's quiet and in a bad mood or talkative and in a good mood.

One forty-five. Everyone rises from the table and goes about their business. Margot and Mother do the washing-up, Mr and Mrs van D. head for the divan, Peter for the attic, Father for his divan, Dussel too, and Anne does her homework.

What comes next is the quietest hour of the day; when they're all asleep, there are no disturbances. To judge by his face, Dussel is dreaming of food. But I don't look at him long, because the time whizzes by and before you know it, it'll be 4.00 p.m. and the pedantic Dr Dussel will be standing with the clock in his hand because I'm one minute late clearing off the table.

Yours, Anne

Dearest Kitty,

A few weeks ago I started writing a story, something I made up from beginning to end, and I've enjoyed it so much that the products of my pen are piling up.

Yours, Anne

Dearest Kitty,

We now continue with a typical day in the Annexe. Since we've already had lunch, it's time to describe dinner.

Mr van Daan. Is served first, and takes a generous portion of whatever he likes. Usually joins in the conversation, never fails to give his opinion. Once he's spoken, his word is final. If anyone dares to suggest otherwise, Mr van D. can put up a good fight. Oh, he can hiss like a cat . . . but I'd rather he didn't. Once you've seen it, you never want to see it again. His opinion is the best, he knows the most about everything. Granted, the man has a good head on his shoulders, but it's swelled to no small degree.

Madame. Actually, the best thing would be to say nothing. Some days, especially when a foul mood is on the way, her face is hard to read. If you analyse the discussions, you realize she's not the subject, but the guilty party! A fact everyone prefers to ignore. Even so, you could call her the instigator. Stirring up trouble, now *that's* what Mrs van Daan calls fun. Stirring up trouble between Mrs Frank and Anne. Margot and Mr Frank aren't quite as easy.

But let's return to the table. Mrs van D. may think she doesn't always get enough, but that's not the case. The choicest potatoes, the tastiest morsel, the tenderest bit of whatever there is, that's Madame's motto. The others can all have their turn, as long as I get the best. (Exactly what she accuses Anne Frank of doing.) Her second watchword is: keep talking. As long as somebody's listening, it doesn't seem to occur to her to wonder whether they're interested. She must think that whatever Mrs van Daan says will interest everyone.

Smile coquettishly, pretend you know everything, offer everyone a piece of advice and mother them – that's sure to make a good impression. But if you take a better look, the good impression fades. One, she's hardworking; two, cheerful; three, coquettish – and sometimes a pretty face. That's Petronella van Daan.

The third diner. Says very little. Young Mr van Daan is usually quiet and hardly makes his presence known. As far as his appetite is concerned, he's a Danaïdean vessel that never gets full. Even after the most substantial meal, he can look you calmly in the eye and claim he could have eaten twice as much.

Number four – Margot. Eats like a bird and doesn't talk at all. She eats only vegetables and fruit. 'Spoiled', in the opinion of the van Daans. 'Too little exercise and fresh air', in ours.

Beside her – Mummy. Has a hearty appetite, does her share of the talking. No one has the impression, as they do with Mrs van Daan, that this is a housewife. What's the difference between the two? Well, Mrs van D. does the cooking and Mother washes up and polishes the furniture.

Numbers six and seven. I won't say much about Father and me. The former is the most modest person at the table. He always looks to see whether the others have been served first. He needs nothing for himself; the best things are for the children. He's goodness personified. Seated next to him is the Annexe's little bundle of nerves.

Dussel. Help yourself, keep your eyes on the food, eat and don't talk. And if you have to say something, then for goodness' sake talk about food. That doesn't lead to quarrels, just to bragging. He consumes enormous portions, and 'no' is not part of his vocabulary, whether the food is good or bad.

Trousers that come up to his chest, a red jacket, black patent-leather slippers and horn-rimmed glasses – that's how he looks when he's at work at the little table, always studying and never progressing. This is interrupted only by his afternoon nap, food and – his favourite spot – the lavatory. Three, four or five times a day there's bound to be someone waiting outside the door, hopping impatiently from one foot to another, trying to hold it in and barely managing. Does Dussel care? Not a whit. From seven-fifteen to seven-thirty, from twelve-thirty to one, from two to two-fifteen, from four to four-fifteen, from six to six-fifteen, from eleven-thirty to twelve. You can set your watch by them; these are the times for his 'regular sessions'. He never deviates or lets himself be swayed by the voices outside the door, begging him to open up before a disaster occurs.

Number nine is not part of our Annexe family, although she does share our house and table. Bep has a healthy appetite. She cleans her plate and isn't choosy. Bep's easy to please and that pleases us. She can be characterized as follows: cheerful, good-humoured, kind and willing.

Dearest Kitty,

A new idea: during meals I talk more to myself than to the others, which has two advantages. First, they're glad they don't have to listen to my continuous chatter, and second, I don't have to get annoyed by their opinions. I don't think my opinions are stupid but other people do, so it's better to keep them to myself. I apply the same tactic when I have to eat something I loathe. I put the dish in front of me, pretend it's delicious, avoid looking at it as much as possible, and it's gone before I've had time to realize what it is. When I get up in the morning, another very disagreeable moment, I leap out of bed, think to myself, 'You'll be slipping back under the covers soon,' walk to the window, take down the black-out screen, sniff at the crack until I feel a bit of fresh air, and I'm awake. I strip the bed as fast as I can so I won't be tempted to get back in. Do you know what Mother calls this sort of thing? The art of living. Isn't that a funny expression?

We've all been a little confused this past week because our dearly beloved Westertoren bells have been carted off to be melted down for the war, so we have no idea of the exact time, either night or day. I still have hopes that they'll come up with a substitute, made of tin or copper or some such thing, to remind the neighbourhood of the clock.

Everywhere I go, upstairs or down, they all cast admiring glances at my feet, which are adorned by a pair of exceptionally beautiful (for times like these!) shoes. Miep managed to snap them up for 27.50 guilders. Burgundy-coloured suede and leather with medium-sized high heels. I feel as if I'm on stilts, and look even taller than I already am.

Yesterday was my unlucky day. I pricked my right thumb with the blunt end of a big needle. As a result, Margot had to peel potatoes for me (take the good with the bad), and writing was awkward. Then I bumped into the cupboard door so hard it nearly knocked me over, and was scolded for making such a racket. They wouldn't let me run water to bathe my forehead, so now I'm walking around with a giant lump over my right eye. To make matters worse, the little toe on my right foot got stuck in the vacuum cleaner. It bled and hurt, but my other ailments were already causing me so much trouble that I let this one slide, which was stupid of me, because now I'm walking around with an infected toe. What with the ointment, the gauze and the tape, I can't get my heavenly new shoe on my foot.

Dussel has put us in danger for the umpteenth time. He actually had Miep bring him a book, an anti-Mussolini tirade, which has been banned. On the way here she was knocked down by an SS motorcycle. She lost her head and shouted 'You brutes!' and went on her way. I don't dare think what would have happened if she'd been taken down to headquarters.

Yours, Anne

A Daily Chore in Our Little Community: Peeling Potatoes!

One person goes to get some newspapers; another, the knives (keeping the best for himself, of course); the third, the potatoes; and the fourth, the water.

Mr Dussel begins. He may not always peel them very well, but he does peel non-stop, glancing left and right to see if everyone is doing it the way he does. No, they're not!

'Look, Anne, I am taking peeler in my hand like so and going from the top to bottom! *Nein*, not so . . . but so!'

'I think my way is easier, Mr Dussel,' I say tentatively.

'But this is best way, Anne. This you can take from me. Of course, it is no matter, you do the way you want.'

We go on peeling. I glance at Dussel out of the corner of my eye. Lost in thought, he shakes his head (over me, no doubt), but says no more.

I keep on peeling. Then I look at Father, on the other

side of me. To Father, peeling potatoes is not a chore, but precision work. When he reads, he has a deep wrinkle in the back of his head. But when he's preparing potatoes, beans or vegetables, he seems to be totally absorbed in his task. He puts on his potato-peeling face, and when it's set in that particular way, it would be impossible for him to turn out anything less than a perfectly peeled potato.

I keep on working. I glance up for a second, but that's all the time I need. Mrs van D. is trying to attract Dussel's attention. She starts by looking in his direction, but Dussel pretends not to notice. She winks, but Dussel goes on peeling. She laughs, but Dussel still doesn't look up. Then Mother laughs too, but Dussel pays them no notice. Having failed to achieve her goal, Mrs van D. is obliged to change tactics. There's a brief silence. Then she says, 'Putti, why don't you put on an apron? Otherwise, I'll have to spend all day tomorrow trying to get the spots out of your suit!'

'I'm not getting it dirty.'

Another brief silence. 'Putti, why don't you sit down?'

'I'm fine this way. I like standing up!'

Silence.

'Putti, look out, *du spritzt schon*!'*

'I know, Mummy, but I'm being careful.'

Mrs van D. casts about for another topic. 'Um, Putti, why aren't the British carrying out any bombing raids today?'

'Because the weather's bad, Kerli!'

'But yesterday it was such nice weather and they weren't flying then either.'

'Let's drop the subject.'

'Why? Can't a person talk about that or offer an opinion?'

'No!'

---

* Now you're splashing!

'Well, why in the world not?'

'Oh, be quiet, *Mammichen*!'*

'Mr Frank always answers *his* wife.'

Mr van D. is trying to control himself. This remark always rubs him up the wrong way, but Mrs van D.'s not one to quit: 'Oh, there's never going to be an invasion!'

Mr van D. goes white, and when she notices it, Mrs van D. turns red, but she's not about to be deterred: 'The British aren't doing a thing!'

The bomb bursts. 'And now shut up, *Donnerwetter noch mal*!'†

Mother can barely stifle a laugh, and I stare straight ahead.

Scenes like these are repeated almost daily, unless they've just had a terrible row. In that case, neither Mr nor Mrs van D. says a word.

It's time for me to get some more potatoes. I go up to the attic, where Peter is busy picking fleas from the cat. He looks up, the cat notices it, and whoosh . . . he's gone. Out of the window and into the rain gutter.

Peter swears; I laugh and slip out of the room.

Freedom in the Annexe

Five-thirty. Bep's arrival signals the beginning of our nightly freedom. Things get going right away. I go upstairs with Bep, who usually has her pudding before the rest of us. The moment she sits down, Mrs van D. begins stating her wishes. Her list usually starts with 'Oh, by the way, Bep, something else I'd like . . .' Bep winks at me. Mrs van D. doesn't miss a chance to make her wishes known to whoever comes

---

* Mummy.
† For crying out loud!

upstairs. It must be one of the reasons none of them likes to go up there.

Five forty-five. Bep leaves. I go down two floors to have a look around: first to the kitchen, then to the private office and then to the coal store to open the cat door for Mouschi.

After a long tour of inspection, I land up in Mr Kugler's office. Mr van Daan is combing all the drawers and files for today's mail. Peter picks up Boche and the warehouse key; Pim lugs the typewriters upstairs; Margot looks around for a quiet place to do her office work; Mrs van D. puts a kettle of water on the gas ring; Mother comes down the stairs with a pan of potatoes; we all know our jobs.

Soon Peter comes back from the warehouse. The first question they ask him is whether he's remembered the bread. No, he hasn't. He crouches before the door to the front office to make himself as small as possible and crawls on his hands and knees to the steel cabinet, takes out the bread and starts to leave. At any rate, that's what he intends to do, but before he knows what's happened, Mouschi has jumped over him and gone to sit under the desk.

Peter looks all around him. Aha, there's the cat! He crawls back into the office and grabs the cat by the tail. Mouschi hisses, Peter sighs. What has he accomplished? Mouschi's now sitting by the window licking herself, very pleased at having escaped Peter's clutches. Peter has no choice but to lure her with a piece of bread. Mouschi takes the bait, follows him out, and the door closes.

I watch the entire scene through a crack in the door.

Mr van Daan is angry and slams the door. Margot and I exchange looks and think the same thing: he must have worked himself into a rage again because of some blunder on Mr Kugler's part, and he's forgotten all about the Keg Company next door.

Another step is heard in the passage. Dussel comes in, goes towards the window with an air of propriety, sniffs . . . coughs, sneezes and clears his throat. He's out of luck – it was pepper. He continues to the front office. The curtains are open, which means he can't get at his writing paper. He disappears with a scowl.

Margot and I exchange another glance. 'One less page for his sweetheart tomorrow,' I hear her say. I nod in agreement.

An elephant's tread is heard on the stairway. It's Dussel, seeking comfort in his favourite spot.

We continue working. Knock, knock, knock . . . Three taps means dinnertime!

MONDAY, 23 AUGUST 1943

Wenn Die Uhr Halb Neune Schlägt . . .*

Margot and Mother are nervous. 'Shh . . . Father. Be quiet, Otto. Shh . . . Pim! It's eight-thirty. Come here, you can't run the water any more. Walk softly!' A sample of what's said to Father in the bathroom. At the stroke of half past eight, he has to be in the living-room. No running water, no flushing toilet, no walking around, no noise whatsoever. As long as the office staff hasn't arrived, sounds travel more easily to the warehouse.

The door opens upstairs at eight-twenty, and this is followed by three gentle taps on the floor . . . Anne's porridge. I clamber up the stairs to get my dog-bowl.

Back downstairs, everything has to be done quickly, quickly: I comb my hair, put away the potty, shove the bed back in place. Quiet! The clock is striking eight-thirty! Mrs

---

* When the clock strikes half past eight.

van D. changes her shoes and shuffles through the room in her slippers; Mr van D. too – a veritable Charlie Chaplin. All is quiet.

The ideal family scene has now reached its high point. I want to read or study and Margot does too. Father and Mother ditto. Father is sitting (with Dickens and the dictionary, of course) on the edge of the sagging, squeaky bed, which doesn't even have a decent mattress. Two bolsters can be piled on top of each other. 'I don't need these,' he thinks. 'I can manage without them!'

Once he starts reading, he doesn't look up. He laughs now and then and tries to get Mother to read a passage.

'I don't have the time right now!'

He looks disappointed, but then continues to read. A little while later, when he comes across another interesting bit, he tries again: 'You *have* to read this, Mother!'

Mother sits on the folding bed, either reading, sewing, knitting or studying, whichever is next on her list. An idea suddenly occurs to her, and she quickly says, so as not to forget, 'Anne, remember to . . . Margot, jot this down . . .'

After a while it's quiet again. Margot slams her book shut; Father knits his forehead, his eyebrows forming a funny curve and his wrinkle of concentration reappearing at the back of his head, and he buries himself in his book again; Mother starts chatting with Margot; and I get curious and listen too. Pim is drawn into the conversation . . . Nine o'clock. Breakfast!

FRIDAY, 10 SEPTEMBER 1943

Dearest Kitty,

Every time I write to you, something special has happened, usually unpleasant rather than pleasant. This time, however, something wonderful is going on.

On Wednesday, 8 September we were listening to the seven o'clock news when we heard an announcement: 'Here is some of the best news of the war so far: Italy has capitulated.' Italy has unconditionally surrendered! The Dutch broadcast from England began at eight-fifteen with the news: 'Listeners, an hour and fifteen minutes ago, just as I finished writing my daily report, we received the wonderful news of Italy's capitulation. I tell you, I never tossed my notes into the wastepaper basket with more delight than I did today!'

'God Save the King', the American national anthem and the Russian 'Internationale' were played. As always, the Dutch programme was uplifting without being too optimistic.

The British have landed in Naples. Northern Italy is occupied by the Germans. The truce was signed on Friday, 3 September, the day the British landed in Italy. The Germans are ranting and raving in all the newspapers at the treachery of Badoglio and the Italian king.

Still, there's bad news as well. It's about Mr Kleiman. As you know, we all like him very much. He's unfailingly cheerful and amazingly brave, despite the fact that he's always ill and in pain and can't eat much or do a lot of walking. 'When Mr Kleiman enters a room, the sun begins to shine,' Mother said recently, and she's absolutely right.

Now it seems he has to go into hospital for a very difficult operation on his stomach, and will have to stay there for at least four weeks. You should have seen him when he said good-bye to us. He acted so normally, as though he were just off to run an errand.

Yours, Anne

Dearest Kitty,

Relationships here in the Annexe are getting worse all the time. We don't dare open our mouths at mealtime (except to slip in a bite of food), because no matter what we say, someone is bound to resent it or take it the wrong way. Mr Voskuijl occasionally comes to visit us. Unfortunately, he's not doing very well. He isn't making it any easier for his family, because his attitude seems to be: what do I care, I'm going to die anyway! When I think how touchy everyone is here, I can just imagine what it must be like at the Voskuijls'.

I've been taking valerian every day to fight the anxiety and depression, but it doesn't stop me from being even more miserable the next day. A good hearty laugh would help more than ten valerian drops, but we've almost forgotten how to laugh. Sometimes I'm afraid my face is going to sag with all this sorrow and that my mouth is going to permanently droop at the corners. The others aren't doing any better. Everyone here is dreading the great terror known as winter.

Another fact that doesn't exactly brighten up our days is that Mr van Maaren, the man who works in the warehouse, is getting suspicious about the Annexe. A person with any brains must have noticed by now that Miep sometimes says she's going to the lab, Bep to the files and Mr Kleiman to the Opekta stores, while Mr Kugler claims the Annexe doesn't belong to this building at all, but to the one next door.

We wouldn't care what Mr van Maaren thought of the situation except that he's known to be unreliable and to possess a high degree of curiosity. He's not one who can be put off with a flimsy excuse.

One day Mr Kugler wanted to be extra cautious, so at

twenty past twelve he put on his coat and went to the chemist round the corner. Less than five minutes later he was back, and he sneaked up the stairs like a thief to visit us. At one-fifteen he started to leave, but Bep met him on the landing and warned him that van Maaren was in the office. Mr Kugler did an about-turn and stayed with us until one-thirty. Then he took off his shoes and went in his stockinged feet (despite his cold) to the front attic and down the other stairway, taking one step at a time to avoid the creaks. It took him fifteen minutes to negotiate the stairs, but he ended up safely in the office after having entered from the outside.

In the meantime, Bep had got rid of van Maaren and come to get Mr Kugler from the Annexe. But he'd already left and at that moment was still tiptoeing down the stairs. What must the passers-by have thought when they saw the manager putting on his shoes outside? Hey, you there, in the socks!

Yours, Anne

WEDNESDAY, 29 SEPTEMBER 1943

Dearest Kitty,

It's Mrs van Daan's birthday. Other than one ration coupon each for cheese, meat and bread, all she received from us was a pot of jam. Her husband, Dussel and the office staff gave her nothing but flowers and also food. Such are the times we live in!

Bep had a nervous fit last week because she had so many errands to do. Ten times a day people were sending her out for something, each time insisting she go right away or go again or that she'd done it all wrong. And when you think that she has her regular office work to do, that Mr Kleiman is ill, that Miep is home with a cold and that Bep herself has a sprained ankle, boyfriend troubles and a grumpy father, it's no wonder she's at the end of her tether. We comforted her and told her that if she'd put her foot down once or twice and say she didn't have the time, the shopping lists would shrink of their own accord.

Saturday there was a big drama, the likes of which have never been seen here before. It started with a discussion of van Maaren and ended in a general argument and tears. Dussel complained to Mother that he was being treated like a leper, that no one was friendly to him and that, after all, he hadn't done anything to deserve it. This was followed by a lot of sweet talk, which luckily Mother didn't fall for this time. She told him we were disappointed in him and that, on more than one occasion, he'd been a source of great annoyance. Dussel promised her the moon, but, as usual, we haven't seen so much as a beam.

There's trouble brewing with the van Daans, I can tell! Father's furious because they're cheating us: they've been holding back meat and other things. Oh, what kind of bombshell is about to burst now? If only I weren't so involved in all these skirmishes! If only I could leave here! They're driving us crazy!

Yours, Anne

SUNDAY, 17 OCTOBER 1943

Dearest Kitty,

Mr Kleiman is back, thank goodness! He looks a bit pale, and yet he cheerfully set off to sell some clothes for Mr van Daan.

The disagreeable fact is that Mr van Daan has run out of money. He lost his last hundred guilders in the warehouse, which is still creating trouble for us: the men are wondering how a hundred guilders could land up in the warehouse on a Monday morning. Suspicion abounds. Meanwhile, the hundred guilders have been stolen. Who's the thief?

But I was talking about the money shortage. Mrs van D. has piles of dresses, coats and shoes, none of which she feels she can do without. Mr van D.'s suit is difficult to shift, and Peter's bike was put up for sale but is back again, since nobody wanted it. But the story doesn't end there. You see, Mrs van. D. is going to have to part with her fur coat. In her opinion, the firm should pay for our upkeep, but that's ridiculous. They just had a flaming row about it and have entered the 'oh, my sweet Putti' and 'darling Kerli' stage of reconciliation.

My mind boggles at the profanity this honourable house has had to endure in the past month. Father walks around with his lips pressed together, and whenever he hears his name, he looks up in alarm, as if he's afraid he'll be called upon to resolve another delicate problem. Mother's so over-wrought her cheeks are blotched with red, Margot complains of headaches, Dussel can't sleep, Mrs van D. frets and fumes all day long, and I've gone completely round the bend. To tell you the truth, I sometimes forget who we're at odds with and who we're not.

The only way to take my mind off it is to study, and I've been doing a lot of that lately.

Yours, Anne

FRIDAY, 29 OCTOBER 1943

My dearest Kitty,

Mr Kleiman is out again: his stomach won't give him a moment's peace. He doesn't even know whether it's stopped bleeding. He came to tell us he wasn't feeling well and was going home, and for the first time he seemed really down.

Mr and Mrs van D. have had more raging battles. The reason is simple: they're broke. They wanted to sell an overcoat and a suit of Mr van D.'s, but were unable to find any buyers. His prices were much too high.

Some time ago Mr Kleiman was talking about a furrier he knows. This gave Mr van D. the idea of selling his wife's fur coat. It's made of rabbit skin, and she's had it for seventeen years. Mrs van D. got 325 guilders for it, an enormous amount. She wanted to keep the money herself to buy new clothes after the war, and it took some doing before Mr van D. could make her understand that it was desperately needed to cover household expenses.

You can't imagine the screaming, shouting, stamping of feet and swearing that went on. It was terrifying. My family stood holding its breath at the bottom of the stairs, in case it might be necessary to drag them apart. All the bickering, tears and nervous tension have become such a stress and strain that I fall into my bed at night crying and thanking my lucky stars that I have half an hour to myself.

I'm doing fine, except I've got no appetite. I keep hearing: 'Goodness, you look awful!' I must admit they're doing their best to keep me fit: they're plying me with dextrose, cod-liver oil, brewer's yeast and calcium. My nerves often get the better of me, especially on Sundays; that's when I really feel miserable. The atmosphere is stifling, sluggish, leaden. Outside, you don't hear a single bird, and a deathly, oppressive silence hangs over the house and clings to me as if it were going to drag me into the deepest regions of the underworld. At times like these, Father, Mother and Margot don't matter to me in the least. I wander from room to room, climb up and down the stairs and feel like a songbird whose wings have been ripped off and who keeps hurling itself against the bars of its dark cage. 'Let me out, where there's fresh air and laughter!' a voice within me cries. I don't even bother to reply any more, but lie down on the divan. Sleep makes the silence and the terrible fear go by more quickly, helps pass the time, since it's impossible to kill it.

Yours, Anne

Dearest Kitty,

To take our minds off matters as well as to develop them, Father ordered a catalogue from a correspondence school. Margot pored through the thick brochure three times without finding anything to her liking and within her budget. Father was easier to satisfy and decided to write and ask for a trial lesson in 'Elementary Latin'. No sooner said than done. The lesson arrived, Margot set to work enthusiastically and decided to take the course, despite the expense. It's much too hard for me, though I'd really like to learn Latin.

To give me a new project as well, Father asked Mr Kleiman for a children's Bible so I could finally learn something about the New Testament.

'Are you planning to give Anne a Bible for Hanukkah?' Margot asked, somewhat perturbed.

'Yes . . . Well, maybe St Nicholas' Day would be a better occasion,' Father replied.

Jesus and Hanukkah don't exactly go together.

Since the vacuum cleaner's broken, I have to take an old brush to the rug every night. The window's closed, the light's on, the stove's burning, and there I am brushing away at the rug. 'That's sure to be a problem,' I thought to myself the first time. 'There're bound to be complaints.' I was right: Mother got a headache from the thick clouds of dust whirling

142

around the room, Margot's new Latin dictionary was caked with dirt, and Pim grumbled that the floor didn't look any different anyway. Small thanks for my pains.

We've decided that from now on the stove is going to be lit at seven-thirty on Sunday mornings instead of five-thirty. I think it's risky. What will the neighbours think of our smoking chimney?

It's the same with the curtains. Ever since we first went into hiding, they've been tacked firmly to the windows. Sometimes one of the ladies or gentlemen can't resist the urge to peek outside. The result: a storm of reproaches. The response: 'Oh, nobody will notice.' That's how every act of carelessness begins and ends. No one will notice, no one will hear, no one will pay the least bit of attention. Easy to say, but is it true?

At the moment, the tempestuous quarrels have subsided; only Dussel and the van Daans are still at loggerheads. When Dussel is talking about Mrs van D., he invariably calls her 'that old bat' or 'that stupid hag', and conversely, Mrs van D. refers to our ever so learned gentleman as an 'old maid' or a 'touchy neurotic spinster', etc.

The pot calling the kettle black!

Yours, Anne

MONDAY EVENING, 8 NOVEMBER 1943

Dearest Kitty,

If you were to read all my letters in one sitting, you'd be struck by the fact that they were written in a variety of moods. It annoys me to be so dependent on the moods here in the Annexe, but I'm not the only one: we're all subject to them. If I'm engrossed in a book, I have to rearrange my thoughts before I can mingle with other people, because otherwise they might think I was strange. As you can see, I'm currently in the middle of a depression. I couldn't really tell you what set it off, but I think it stems from my cowardice, which confronts me at every turn. This evening, when Bep was still here, the doorbell rang long and loud. I instantly turned white, my stomach churned, and my heart beat wildly – and all because I was afraid.

At night in bed I see myself alone in a dungeon, without Father and Mother. Or I'm roaming the streets, or the Annexe is on fire, or they come in the middle of the night to take us away and I crawl under my bed in desperation. I see everything as if it were actually taking place. And to think it might all happen soon!

Miep often says she envies us because we have such peace and quiet here. That may be true, but she's obviously not thinking about our fear.

I simply can't imagine the world will ever be normal again for us. I do talk about 'after the war', but it's as if I were talking about a castle in the air, something that can never come true.

I see the eight of us in the Annexe as if we were a patch of blue sky surrounded by menacing black clouds. The perfectly round spot on which we're standing is still safe, but the clouds are moving in on us, and the ring between us and the approaching danger is being pulled tighter and tighter. We're surrounded by darkness and danger, and in our desperate search for a way out we keep bumping into each other. We look at the fighting down below and the peace and beauty up above. In the meantime, we've been cut off by the dark mass of clouds, so that we can go neither up nor down. It looms before us like an impenetrable wall, trying to crush us, but not yet able to. I can only cry out and implore, 'Oh, ring, ring, open wide and let us out!'

Yours, Anne

Dearest Kitty,

I have a good title for this chapter:

Ode to My Fountain Pen
In Memoriam

My fountain pen was always one of my most prized possessions; I valued it highly, especially because it had a thick nib, and I can only write neatly with thick nibs. It has led a long and interesting fountain-pen life, which I will summarize below.

When I was nine, my fountain pen (packed in cotton wool) arrived as a 'sample of no commercial value' all the way from Aachen, where my grandmother (the kindly donor) used to live. I lay in bed with flu, while the February winds howled around our flat. This splendid fountain pen came in a red leather case, and I showed it to my girlfriends the first chance I got. Me, Anne Frank, the proud owner of a fountain pen.

When I was ten, I was allowed to take the pen to school, and to my surprise, the teacher even let me write with it. When I was eleven, however, my treasure had to be tucked away again, because my sixth-form teacher allowed us to use only school pens and ink-pots. When I was twelve, I started at the Jewish Lyceum and my fountain pen was given a new case in honour of the occasion. Not only did it have room for a pencil, it also had a zip, which was much more impressive. When I was thirteen, the fountain pen went with me to the Annexe, and together we've raced through countless diaries and compositions. I'd turned fourteen and my fountain pen was enjoying the last year of its life with me when . . .

It was just after five on Friday afternoon. I came out of my room and was about to sit down at the table to write when I was roughly pushed to one side to make room for Margot and Father, who wanted to practise their Latin. The fountain pen remained unused on the table, while its owner, sighing, was forced to make do with a very tiny corner of the table, where she began rubbing beans. That's how we remove mould from the beans and restore them to their original state. At a quarter to six I swept the floor, dumped the dirt into a newspaper, along with the rotten beans, and tossed it into the stove. A giant flame shot up, and I thought it was wonderful that the stove, which had been gasping its last breath, had made such a miraculous recovery.

All was quiet again. The Latin students had left, and I sat down at the table to pick up where I'd left off. But no matter where I looked, my fountain pen was nowhere in sight. I took another look. Margot looked, Mother looked, Father looked, Dussel looked. But it had vanished.

'Maybe it fell in the stove, along with the beans!' Margot suggested.

'No, it couldn't have!' I replied.

But that evening, when my fountain pen still hadn't turned up, we all assumed it had been burned, especially because celluloid is highly inflammable. Our darkest fears were confirmed the next day when Father went to empty the stove and discovered the clip, used to fasten it to a pocket, among the ashes. Not a trace of the gold nib was left. 'It must have melted into stone,' Father conjectured.

I'm left with one consolation, small though it may be: my fountain pen was cremated, just as I would like to be some day.

Yours, Anne

Dearest Kitty,

Recent events have the house rocking on its foundations. Owing to an outbreak of diphtheria at Bep's, she won't be allowed to come in contact with us for six weeks. Without her, the cooking and shopping will be very difficult, not to mention how much we'll miss her company. Mr Kleiman is still in bed and has eaten nothing but gruel for three weeks. Mr Kugler is up to his neck in work.

Margot sends her Latin lessons to a teacher, who corrects and then returns them. She's registered under Bep's name. The teacher's very nice, and witty too. I bet he's glad to have such a clever pupil.

Dussel is in a turmoil and we don't know why. It all began with Dussel's saying nothing when he was upstairs; he didn't exchange so much as a word with either Mr or Mrs van Daan. We all noticed it. This went on for a few days, and then Mother took the opportunity to warn him about Mrs van D., who could make life miserable for him. Dussel said Mr van Daan had started the silent treatment and he had no intention of breaking it. I should explain that yesterday was 16 November, the first anniversary of his living in the Annexe. Mother received a plant in honour of the occasion, but Mrs van Daan, who had alluded to the date for weeks and made no bones about the fact that she thought Dussel should treat us to dinner, received nothing. Instead of making use of the opportunity to thank us – for the first time – for unselfishly taking him in, he didn't utter a word. And on the morning of the sixteenth, when I asked him whether I should offer him my congratulations or my condolences, he replied that either one would do. Mother, having cast herself in the role of peacemaker, made no headway whatsoever, and the situation finally ended in a draw.

I can say without exaggeration that Dussel has definitely got a screw loose. We often laugh to ourselves because he has no memory, no fixed opinions and no common sense. He's amused us more than once by trying to pass on the news he's just heard, since the message invariably gets garbled in transmission. Furthermore, he answers every reproach or accusation with a load of fine promises, which he never manages to keep.

> *'Der Mann hat einen grossen Geist*
> *Und ist so klein von Taten!'* *

Yours, Anne

SATURDAY, 27 NOVEMBER 1943

Dearest Kitty,

Last night, just as I was falling asleep, Hanneli suddenly appeared before me.

I saw her there, dressed in rags, her face thin and worn. She looked at me with such sadness and reproach in her enormous eyes that I could read the message in them: 'Oh, Anne, why have you deserted me? Help me, help me, rescue me from this hell!'

And I can't help her. I can only stand by and watch while other people suffer and die. All I can do is pray to God to bring her back to us. I saw Hanneli, and no one else, and I understood why. I misjudged her, wasn't mature enough to understand how difficult it was for her. She was devoted to

---

* A well-known expression: 'The spirit of the man is great, / How puny are his deeds.'

her friend, and it must have seemed as though I were try-ing to take her away. The poor thing, she must have felt aw-ful! I know, because I recognize the feeling in myself! I had an occasional flash of understanding, but then got selfishly wrapped up again in my own problems and pleasures.

It was horrible of me to treat her that way, and now she was looking at me, oh so helplessly, with her pale face and beseeching eyes. If only I could help her! Dear God, I have everything I could wish for, while fate has her in its deadly clutches. She was as devout as I am, maybe even more so, and she too wanted to do what was right. But then why have I been chosen to live, while she's probably going to die? What's the difference between us? Why are we now so far apart?

To be honest, I hadn't thought of her for months – no, for at least a year. I hadn't forgotten her entirely, and yet it wasn't until I saw her before me that I thought of all her suffering.

Oh, Hanneli, I hope that if you live to the end of the war and return to us, I'll be able to take you in and make up for the wrong I've done you.

But even if I were ever in a position to help, she wouldn't need it more than she does now. I wonder if she ever thinks of me, and what she's feeling?

Merciful God, comfort her, so that at least she won't be alone. Oh, if only You could tell her I'm thinking of her with compassion and love, it might help her go on.

I've got to stop dwelling on this. It won't get me anywhere. I keep seeing her enormous eyes, and they haunt me. Does Hanneli really and truly believe in God, or has religion merely been foisted upon her? I don't even know that. I never took the trouble to ask.

Hanneli, Hanneli, if only I could take you away, if only I could share everything I have with you. It's too late. I can't help, or undo the wrong I've done. But I'll never forget her again and I'll always pray for her!

Yours, Anne

Dearest Kitty,

The closer it got to St Nicholas' Day, the more we all thought back to last year's festively decorated basket. More than anyone, I thought it would be terrible to skip a celebration this year. After long deliberation, I finally came up with an idea, something funny. I consulted Pim, and a week ago we set to work writing a verse for each person.

Sunday evening at a quarter to eight we trooped upstairs carrying the big laundry basket, which had been decorated with cutouts and bows made of pink and blue carbon paper. On top was a large piece of brown wrapping paper with a note attached. Everyone was rather amazed at the sheer size of the gift. I removed the note and read it aloud:

> *'Once again St Nicholas' Day*
> *Has even come to our hideaway;*
> *It won't be quite as fun, I fear,*
> *As the happy day we had last year.*
> *Then we were hopeful, no reason to doubt*
> *That optimism would win the bout,*
> *And by the time this year came round,*
> *We'd all be free, and safe and sound.*
> *Still, let's not forget it's St Nicholas' Day,*
> *Though we've nothing left to give away.*
> *We'll have to find something else to do:*
> *So everyone please look in their shoe!'*

As each person took their own shoe out of the basket,

there was a roar of laughter. Inside each shoe was a little paper parcel addressed to its owner.

Yours, Anne

Dearest Kitty,

A bad case of flu has prevented me from writing to you until today. Being ill here is dreadful. With every cough, I had to duck under the blanket – once, twice, three times – and try to keep from coughing any more. Most of the time the tickle refused to go away, so I had to drink milk with honey, sugar or cough drops. I get dizzy just thinking about all the cures I've been subjected to: sweating out the fever, steam treatment, wet compresses, dry compresses, hot drinks, swabbing my throat, lying still, heating pad, hot-water bottles, lemonade and, every two hours, the thermometer. Will these remedies really make you better? The worst part was when Mr Dussel decided to play doctor and lay his pomaded head on my bare chest to listen to the sounds. Not only did his hair tickle, but I was embarrassed, even though he went to school thirty years ago and does have some kind of medical degree. Why should he lay his head on my heart? After all, he's not my boyfriend! For that matter, he wouldn't be able to tell a healthy sound from an unhealthy one. He'd have to have his ears cleaned first, since he's becoming alarmingly hard of hearing. But enough about my illness. I'm fit as a fiddle again. I've grown almost half an inch and gained two pounds. I'm pale, but itching to get back to my books.

*Ausnahmsweise** (the only word that will do here), we're

---

* By way of exception.

all getting on well together. No squabbles, though that probably won't last long. There hasn't been such peace and quiet in this house for at least six months.

Bep is still in isolation, but any day now her sister will no longer be contagious.

For Christmas, we're getting extra cooking oil, sweets and treacle. For Hanukkah, Mr Dussel gave Mrs van Daan and Mother a beautiful cake, which he'd asked Miep to bake. On top of all the work she has to do! Margot and I received a brooch made out of a penny, all bright and shiny. I can't really describe it, but it's lovely.

I also have a Christmas present for Miep and Bep. For a whole month I've saved up the sugar I put on my porridge, and Mr Kleiman has used it to have fondant made.

The weather is drizzly and overcast, the stove stinks, and the food lies heavily on our stomachs, producing a variety of rumbles.

The war is at an impasse, spirits are low.

Yours, Anne

FRIDAY, 24 DECEMBER 1943

Dear Kitty,

As I've written many times before, moods have a tendency to affect us quite a bit here, and in my case it's been getting worse lately. '*Himmelhoch jauchzend, zu Tode betrübt*'* certainly applies to me. I'm 'on top of the world' when I think of how fortunate we are and compare myself to other Jewish children, and 'in the depths of despair' when, for example, Mrs Kleiman comes by and talks about Jopie's

---

* A famous line from Goethe: 'On top of the world, or in the depths of despair.'

Friday evening, for the first time in my life, I received a Christmas present. Mr Kleiman, Mr Kugler and the girls had prepared a wonderful surprise for us. Miep made a delicious Christmas cake with 'Peace 1944' written on top, and Bep provided biscuits that were up to pre-war standards.

There was a pot of yoghurt for Peter, Margot and me, and a bottle of beer for each of the adults. And once again everything was wrapped so nicely, with pretty pictures glued to the parcels. For the rest, the holidays passed by quickly for us.

Anne

I was very sad again last night. Grandma and Hanneli came to me once more. Grandma, oh, my sweet Grandma. How little we understood what she suffered, how kind she always was and what an interest she took in everything that concerned us. And to think that all that time she was carefully guarding her terrible secret.*

Grandma was always so loyal and good. She would never have let any of us down. Whatever happened, no matter how much I misbehaved, Grandma always stuck up for me. Grandma, did you love me, or did you not understand me either? I don't know. How lonely Grandma must have been, in spite of us. You can be lonely even when you're loved by many people, since you're still not anybody's 'one and only'.

And Hanneli? Is she still alive? What's she doing? Dear

---

* Anne's grandmother was terminally ill.

God, watch over her and bring her back to us. Hanneli, you're a reminder of what my fate might have been. I keep seeing myself in your place. So why am I often miserable about what goes on here? Shouldn't I be happy, contented and glad, except when I'm thinking of Hanneli and those suffering along with her? I'm selfish and cowardly. Why do I always think and dream the most awful things and want to scream in terror? Because, in spite of everything, I still don't have enough faith in God. He's given me so much, which I don't deserve, and yet each day I make so many mistakes!

Thinking about the suffering of those you hold dear can reduce you to tears; in fact, you could spend the whole day crying. The most you can do is pray for God to perform a miracle and save at least some of them. And I hope I'm doing enough of that!

Anne

THURSDAY, 30 DECEMBER 1943

Dearest Kitty,

Since the last raging quarrels, things have settled down here, not only between ourselves, Dussel and 'upstairs', but also between Mr and Mrs van D. Nevertheless, a few dark thunderclouds are heading this way, and all because of . . . food. Mrs van D. came up with the ridiculous idea of frying fewer potatoes in the morning and saving them for later in the day. Mother and Dussel and the rest of us didn't agree with her, so now we're dividing up the potatoes as well. It seems the fats and oils aren't being doled out fairly, and Mother's going to have to put a stop to it. I'll let you know if there are any interesting developments. For the last few months now we've been splitting up the meat (theirs with fat, ours without), the soup (they eat it, we don't), the potatoes (theirs peeled, ours not), the extras and now the fried potatoes too.

If only we could split up completely!

Yours, Anne

PS. Bep had a picture postcard of the entire Royal Family copied for me. Juliana looks very young, and so does the Queen. The three little girls are adorable. It was incredibly nice of Bep, don't you think?

SUNDAY, 2 JANUARY 1944

Dearest Kitty,

This morning, when I had nothing to do, I leafed through the pages of my diary and came across so many letters dealing with the subject of 'Mother' in such strong terms that I was shocked. I said to myself, 'Anne, is that really you talking about hate? Oh, Anne, how could you?'

I continued to sit with the open book in my hand and wonder why I was filled with so much anger and hate that I had to confide it all to you. I tried to understand the Anne of last year and make apologies for her, because as long as I leave you with these accusations and don't attempt to explain what prompted them, my conscience won't be clear. I was suffering then (and still do) from moods that kept my head under water (figuratively speaking) and allowed me to see things only from my own perspective, without calmly considering what the others – those whom I, with my mercurial temperament, had hurt or offended – had said, and then behaving as they would have done.

I hid inside myself, thought of no one but myself and calmly wrote down all my joy, sarcasm and sorrow in my diary. Because this diary has become a kind of scrapbook, it means a great deal to me, but I could easily write 'over and done with' on many of its pages.

I was furious at Mother (and still am a lot of the time). It's true, she didn't understand me, but I didn't understand her either. Because she loved me, she was tender and affectionate, but because of the difficult situations I put her in, and the sad circumstances in which she found herself, she was nervous and irritable, so I can understand why she was often short with me.

I was offended, took it far too much to heart and was insolent and beastly to her, which, in turn, made her unhappy. We were caught in a vicious circle of unpleasantness and sorrow. Not a very happy period for either of us, but at least it's coming to an end. I didn't want to see what was going on, and I felt very sorry for myself, but that's understandable too.

Those violent outbursts on paper are simply expressions of anger that, in normal life, I could have worked off by locking myself in my room and stamping my foot a few times or calling Mother names behind her back.

The period of tearfully passing judgement on Mother is over. I've grown wiser and Mother's nerves are a bit steadier. Most of the time I manage to hold my tongue when I'm annoyed, and she does too; so on the surface, we seem to be getting along better. But there's one thing I can't do, and that's to love Mother with the devotion of a child.

I soothe my conscience with the thought that it's better for unkind words to be down on paper than for Mother to have to carry them around in her heart.

Yours, Anne

Dearest Kitty,

Today I have two things to confess. It's going to take a long time, but I have to tell them to someone, and you're the most likely candidate, since I know you'll keep a secret, no matter what happens.

The first is about Mother. As you know, I've frequently complained about her and then tried my best to be nice. I've suddenly realized what's wrong with her. Mother has said that she sees us more as friends than as daughters. That's all very nice, of course, except that a friend can't take the place of a mother. I need my mother to set a good example and be a person I can respect, but in most matters she's an example of what *not* to do. I have the feeling that Margot thinks so differently about these things that she'd never be able to understand what I've just told you. And Father avoids all conversations having to do with Mother.

I imagine a mother as a woman who, first and foremost, possesses a great deal of tact, especially towards her adolescent children, and not one who, like Mumsie, pokes fun at me when I cry. Not because I'm in pain, but because of other things.

This may seem trivial, but there's one incident I've never forgiven her for. It happened one day when I had to go to the dentist. Mother and Margot planned to go with me and agreed I should take my bicycle. When the dentist was finished and we were back outside, Margot and Mother very sweetly informed me that they were going into town to buy or look at something, I don't remember what, and of course I wanted to go along. But they said I couldn't come because I had my bike with me. Tears of rage rushed to my eyes, and Margot and Mother began laughing at me. I was so furious that I stuck my tongue out at them, right there on the street. A little old lady happened to be passing by, and she looked terribly shocked. I cycled home and must have cried for hours. Strangely enough, even though Mother has wounded me thousands of times, this particular wound still stings whenever I think of how angry I was.

I find it difficult to confess the second one because it's about myself. I'm not prudish, Kitty, and yet every time they give a blow-by-blow account of their trips to the lavatory, which they often do, my whole body rises in revolt.

Yesterday I read an article on blushing by Sis Heyster. It was as if she'd addressed it directly to me. Not that I blush easily, but the rest of the article did apply. What she basically says is that during puberty girls withdraw into themselves and begin thinking about the wondrous changes taking place in their bodies. I feel that too, which probably accounts for my recent embarrassment over Margot, Mother and Father. On the other hand, Margot is a lot shyer than I am, and yet she's not in the least embarrassed.

I think that what's happening to me is so wonderful, and I don't just mean the changes taking place on the outside of my body, but also those on the inside. I never discuss myself or any of these things with others, which is why I have to talk about them to myself. Whenever I have my period (and that's only been three times), I have the feeling that in spite of all the pain, discomfort and mess, I'm carrying around a sweet secret. So even though it's a nuisance, in a certain way I'm always looking forward to the time when I'll feel that secret inside me once again.

Sis Heyster also writes that girls my age feel very insecure about themselves and are just beginning to discover that they're individuals with their own ideas, thoughts and habits. I'd just turned thirteen when I came here, so I started thinking about myself and realized that I've become an 'independent person' sooner than most girls. Sometimes when I lie in bed at night I feel a terrible urge to touch my breasts and listen to the quiet, steady beating of my heart.

Unconsciously, I had these feelings even before I came here. Once when I was spending the night at Jacque's, I could no longer restrain my curiosity about her body, which she'd always hidden from me and which I'd never seen. I asked her whether, as proof of our friendship, we could touch each other's breasts. Jacque refused. I also had a terrible desire to kiss her, which I did. Every time I see a female nude, such as the Venus in my art history book, I go into ecstasy. Sometimes I find them so exquisite I have to struggle to hold back my tears. If only I had a girlfriend!

THURSDAY, 6 JANUARY 1944

Dearest Kitty,

My longing for someone to talk to has become so unbearable that I somehow took it into my head to select Peter for this role. On the few occasions when I have gone to Peter's room during the day, I've always thought it was nice and cosy. But Peter's too polite to show someone the door when they're bothering him, so I've never dared to stay long. I've always been afraid he'd think I was a pest. I've been looking for an excuse to linger in his room and get him talking without his noticing, and yesterday I got my chance. Peter, you see, is currently going through a crossword-puzzle craze, and he doesn't do anything else all day. I was helping him, and we soon ended up sitting across from each other at his table, Peter on the chair and me on the divan.

It gave me a wonderful feeling when I looked into his dark blue eyes and saw how bashful my unexpected visit had made him. I could read his innermost thoughts, and in his face I saw a look of helplessness and uncertainty as to how to behave, and at the same time a flicker of awareness of his masculinity. I saw his shyness, and I melted. I wanted to say, 'Tell me about yourself. Look beneath my chatty exterior.' But I found that it was easier to think up questions than to ask them.

The evening came to a close, and nothing happened, except that I told him about the article on blushing. Not what I wrote you, of course, just that he would grow more secure as he got older.

That night I lay in bed and cried my eyes out, all the while making sure no one could hear me. The idea that I had to beg Peter for favours was simply revolting. But people will do almost anything to satisfy their longings; take me, for example, I've made up my mind to visit Peter more often and, somehow, get him to talk to me.

You mustn't think I'm in love with Peter, because I'm not. If the van Daans had had a daughter instead of a son, I'd have tried to make friends with her.

This morning I woke up just before seven and immediately remembered what I'd been dreaming about. I was sitting on a chair and across from me was Peter . . . Peter Schiff. We were looking at Mary Bos's sketchbook. The dream was so vivid I can even remember some of the drawings. But that wasn't all – the dream went on. Peter's eyes suddenly met mine, and I stared for a long time into those velvety brown eyes. Then he said very softly, 'If I'd only known, I'd have come to you long ago!' I turned abruptly away, overcome by emotion. And then I felt a soft, oh-so-cool and gentle cheek against mine, and it felt so good, so good . . .

At that point I woke up, still feeling his cheek against mine and his brown eyes staring deep into my heart, so deep that he could read how much I'd loved him and how much I still do. Again my eyes filled with tears, and I was sad because I'd lost him once more, and yet at the same time glad because I knew with certainty that Peter is still the only one for me.

It's funny, but I often have such vivid images in my dreams. One night I saw Grammy* so clearly that I could even make out her skin of soft, crinkly velvet. Another time Grandma appeared to me as a guardian angel. After that it was Hanneli, who still symbolizes to me the suffering of my friends as well as that of Jews in general, so that when I'm praying for her, I'm also praying for all the Jews and all those in need.

And now Peter, my dearest Peter. I've never had such a clear mental image of him. I don't need a photograph, I can see him oh so well.

Yours, Anne

FRIDAY, 7 JANUARY 1944

Dearest Kitty,

I'm such an idiot. I forgot that I haven't yet told you the story of my one true love.

When I was a little girl, way back in nursery school, I took a liking to Sally Kimmel. His father was gone, and he and his mother lived with an aunt. One of Sally's cousins was a good-looking, slender, dark-haired boy named Appy, who later turned out to look like a matinée idol and aroused more admiration than the short, comical, chubby Sally. For a long time we went everywhere together, but aside from

---

* Grammy is Anne's grandmother on her father's side, and Grandma her grandmother on her mother's side.

that, my love was unrequited until Peter crossed my path. I had an absolute crush on him. He liked me too, and we were inseparable for one whole summer. I can still see us walking hand in hand through our neighbourhood, Peter in a white cotton suit and me in a short summer dress. At the end of the summer holidays he moved up a form to the next school, while I stayed in the sixth form. He'd collect me on the way home, or I'd pick him up. Peter was the ideal boy: tall, slim and good-looking, with a serious, quiet and intelligent face. He had dark hair, beautiful brown eyes, ruddy cheeks and a nicely pointed nose. I was crazy about his smile, which made him look so boyish and mischievous.

I'd gone to the country during the summer holidays, and when I came back, Peter was no longer at his old address; he'd moved and was living with a much older boy, who apparently told him I was just a child, because Peter stopped seeing me. I loved him so much that I didn't want to face the truth. I kept clinging to him until the day I finally realized that if I continued to chase after him, people would say I was mad about boys.

The years went by. Peter went around with girls his own age and no longer bothered to say hello to me. I started school at the Jewish Lyceum, and several boys in my class were in love with me. I enjoyed it and felt honoured by their attentions, but that was all. Later on, Hello had a terrible crush on me, but as I've already told you, I never fell in love again.

There's a saying: 'Time heals all wounds.' That's how it was with me. I told myself I'd forgotten Peter and no longer liked him in the least. But my memories of him were so strong that I had to admit to myself that the only reason I no longer liked him was that I was jealous of the other girls. This morning I realized that nothing has changed; on the contrary, as I've grown older and more mature, my love has grown along with me. I can understand now that Peter thought I was childish, and yet it still hurts to think he'd forgotten me completely. I saw his face so clearly; I knew for certain that no one but Peter could have stuck in my mind that way.

I've been in an utter state of confusion today. When Father kissed me this morning, I wanted to shout, 'Oh, if only you were Peter!' I've been thinking of him constantly, and all day long I've been repeating to myself, 'Oh, Petel, my darling, darling Petel . . .'

Where can I find help? I simply have to go on living and praying to God that, if we ever get out of here, Peter's path will cross mine and he'll gaze into my eyes, read the love in them and say, 'Oh, Anne, if I'd only known, I'd have come to you long ago.'

Once when Father and I were talking about sex, he said I was too young to understand that kind of desire. But I thought I did understand it, and now I'm sure I do. Nothing is as dear to me now as my darling Petel!

I saw my face in the mirror, and it looked so different. My eyes were clear and deep, my cheeks were rosy, which they hadn't been in weeks, my mouth was much softer. I looked happy, and yet there was something so sad in my expression that the smile immediately faded from my lips. I'm not happy, since I know Petel's not thinking of me, and yet I can still feel his beautiful eyes gazing at me and his cool, soft cheek against mine . . . Oh, Petel, Petel, how am I ever going to free myself from your image? Wouldn't anyone who took your place be a poor substitute? I love you, with a love so great that it simply couldn't keep growing inside my heart, but had to leap out and reveal itself in all its magnitude.

A week ago, even a day ago, if you'd asked me, 'Which of your friends do you think you'd be most likely to marry?' I'd have answered, 'Sally, since he makes me feel good, peaceful and safe!' But now I'd cry, 'Petel, because I love him with all my heart and all my soul. I surrender myself completely!' Except for that one thing: he may touch my face, but that's as far as it goes.

This morning I imagined I was in the front attic with Petel, sitting on the floor by the windows, and after talking for a while, we both began to cry. Moments later I felt his mouth and his wonderful cheek! Oh, Petel, come to me. Think of me, my dearest Petel!

WEDNESDAY, 12 JANUARY 1944

Dearest Kitty,

Bep's been back for the last two weeks, though her sister won't be allowed back at school until next week. Bep herself spent two days in bed with a bad cold. Miep and Jan were also out for two days, with upset stomachs.

I'm currently going through a dance and ballet craze and am diligently practising my dance steps every evening. I've made an ultra-modern dance costume out of a lacy lavender petticoat belonging to Mumsie. Tape is threaded through the top and tied just above the bust. A pink corded ribbon completes the ensemble. I tried to turn my gym shoes into ballet slippers, but with no success. My stiff limbs are well on the way to becoming as supple as they used to be. A terrific exercise is to sit on the floor, place a heel in each hand and raise both legs in the air. I have to sit on a cushion, because otherwise my poor backside really takes a beating.

Everyone here is reading a book called *A Cloudless Morning*. Mother thought it was extremely good because it with us. We'll somehow get hold of a bag of wood shavings, so we can sleep on the floor. Let's ask Miep and Kleiman to bring some blankets, just in case. And we'll order some extra grain to supplement the sixty-five pounds we already have. Jan can try to find some more beans. At the moment we've got about sixty-five pounds of beans and ten pounds of split peas. And don't forget the fifty tins of vegetables.'

'What about the rest, Mother? Give us the latest figures.'

'Ten tins of fish, forty tins of milk, twenty pounds of powdered milk, three bottles of oil, four pots of butter, four jars of meat, two big jars of strawberries, two jars of raspberries, twenty jars of tomatoes, ten pounds of oatmeal, nine pounds of rice. That's it.'

Our supplies are holding out fairly well. All the same, we have to feed the office staff, which means dipping into our reserves every week, so it's not as much as it seems. We have enough coal and firewood, candles too.

'Let's all make little moneybags to hide in our clothes so we can take our money with us if we need to leave here.'

'We can make lists of what to take first in case we have to run for it, and pack our rucksacks in advance.'

'When the time comes, we'll put two people on look-out, one in the loft at the front of the house and one at the back.'

'Hang on, what's the use of so much food if there isn't any water, gas or electricity?'

'We'll have to cook on the stove. Filter the water and boil it. We should clean some big jugs and fill them with water. We can also store water in the three pans we use for preserving, and in the tin bath.'

'Besides, we still have about two hundred and thirty pounds of winter potatoes in the spice storeroom.'

All day long that's all I hear. Invasion, invasion, nothing but invasion. Arguments about going hungry, dying, bombs, fire extinguishers, sleeping bags, identity cards, poison gas, etc., etc. Not exactly cheerful.

A good example of the explicit warnings of the male contingent is the following conversation with Jan:

Annexe: 'We're afraid that when the Germans retreat, they'll take the entire population with them.'

Jan: 'That's impossible. They haven't got enough trains.'

Annexe: 'Trains? Do you really think they'd put civilians on trains? Absolutely not. Everyone would have to hoof it.' (Or, as Dussel always says, *per pedes apostolorum*.)

Jan: 'I can't believe that. You're always looking on the dark side. What reason would they have to round up all the civilians and take them along?'

Annexe: 'Don't you remember Goebbels saying that if the Germans have to go, they'll slam the doors to all the occupied territories behind them?'

Jan: 'They've said a lot of things.'

Annexe: 'Do you think the Germans are too noble or humane to do it? Their reasoning is: if we go under, we'll drag everyone else down with us.'

Jan: 'You can say what you like, I just don't believe it.'

Annexe: 'It's always the same old story. No one wants to see the danger until it's staring them in the face.'

Jan: 'But you don't know anything for sure. You're just making an assumption.'

Annexe: 'Because we've already been through it all ourselves. First in Germany and then here. What do you think's happening in Russia?'

Jan: 'You shouldn't include the Jews. I don't think anyone knows what's going on in Russia. The British and the Russians are probably exaggerating for propaganda purposes, just like the Germans.'

Annexe: 'Absolutely not. The BBC has always told the

truth. And even if the news is slightly exaggerated, the facts are bad enough as they are. You can't deny that millions of peace-loving citizens in Poland and Russia have been murdered or gassed.'

I'll spare you the rest of our conversations. I'm very calm and take no notice of all the fuss. I've reached the point where I hardly care whether I live or die. The world will keep on turning without me, and I can't do anything to change events anyway. I'll just let matters take their course and concentrate on studying and hope that everything will be all right in the end.

Yours, Anne

TUESDAY, 8 FEBRUARY 1944

Dear Kitty,

I can't tell you how I feel. One minute I'm longing for peace and quiet, and the next for a little fun. We've forgotten how to laugh – I mean, laughing so hard you can't stop.

This morning I had the giggles; you know, the kind we used to have at school. Margot and I were giggling like real teenagers.

Last night there was another scene with Mother. Margot was tucking her woollen blanket around her when suddenly she leapt out of bed and carefully examined the blanket. What do you think she found? A pin! Mother had patched the blanket and forgotten to take it out. Father shook his head meaningfully and made a comment about how careless Mother is. Soon afterwards Mother came in from the bathroom, and just to tease her I said, *'Du bist doch eine echte Rabenmutter.'**

---

* Oh, you *are* cruel.

Of course, she asked me why I'd said that, and we told her about the pin she'd overlooked. She immediately assumed her haughtiest expression and said, 'You're a fine one to talk. When you're sewing, the entire floor is covered with pins. And look, you've left the manicure set lying around again. You never put that away either!'

I said I hadn't used it, and Margot backed me up, since she was the guilty party.

Mother went on talking about how messy I was until I got fed up and said, rather curtly, 'I wasn't even the one who said you were careless. I'm always getting blamed for other people's mistakes!'

Mother fell silent, and less than a minute later I was obliged to kiss her good night. This incident may not have been very important, but these days everything gets on my nerves.

Anne Mary Frank

SATURDAY, 12 FEBRUARY 1944

Dearest Kitty,

The sun is shining, the sky is deep blue, there's a magnificent breeze, and I'm longing – really longing – for everything: conversation, freedom, friends, being alone. I long . . . to cry! I feel as if I were about to explode. I know crying would help, but I can't cry. I'm restless. I walk from one room to another, breathe through the crack in the window frame, feel my heart beating as if to say, 'Fulfil my longing at last . . .'

I think spring is inside me. I feel spring awakening, I feel it in my entire body and soul. I have to force myself to act normally. I'm in a state of utter confusion, don't know what to read, what to write, what to do. I only know that I'm longing for something . . .

Yours, Anne

Dearest Kitty,

A lot has changed for me since Saturday. What's happened is this: I was longing for something (and still am), but . . . a small, a very small, part of the problem has been resolved.

On Sunday morning I noticed, to my great joy (I'll be honest with you), that Peter kept looking at me. Not in the usual way. I don't know, I can't explain it, but I suddenly had the feeling he wasn't as in love with Margot as I used to think. All day long I tried not to look at him too much, because whenever I did, I caught him looking at me and then – well, it made me feel wonderful inside, and that's not a feeling I should have too often.

Sunday evening everyone, except Pim and me, was clustered round the radio, listening to the 'Immortal Music of the German Masters'. Dussel kept twisting and turning the knobs, which annoyed Peter, and the others too. After restraining himself for half an hour, Peter asked somewhat irritably if he would stop fiddling with the radio. Dussel replied in his haughtiest tone, '*Ich mach' das schon!*'* Peter became angry and made an insolent remark. Mr van Daan sided with him, and Dussel had to back down. That was it.

The reason for the disagreement wasn't particularly interesting in and of itself, but Peter has apparently taken the matter very much to heart, because this morning, when I was rummaging around in the crate of books in the attic, Peter came up and began telling me what had happened. I didn't know anything about it, but Peter soon realized he'd found an attentive listener and started warming to his subject.

'Well, it's like this,' he said. 'I don't usually talk much,

---

* I'll decide that.

since I know beforehand I'll just be tongue-tied. I start stuttering and blushing and I twist my words around so much I finally have to stop, because I can't find the right words. That's what happened yesterday. I meant to say something entirely different, but once I started, I got all mixed up. It's awful. I used to have a bad habit, and sometimes I wish I still did: whenever I was angry with someone, I'd beat them up instead of arguing with them. I know this method won't get me anywhere, and that's why I admire you. You're never at a loss for words: you say exactly what you want to say and aren't in the least bit shy.'

'Oh, you're wrong about that,' I replied. 'Most of what I say comes out very differently from the way I'd planned. Plus I talk too much and too long, and that's just as bad.'

'Maybe, but you have the advantage that no one can see you're embarrassed. You don't blush or go to pieces.'

I couldn't help being secretly amused at his words. However, since I wanted him to go on talking quietly about himself, I hid my laughter, sat down on a cushion on the floor, wrapped my arms around my knees and gazed at him intently.

I'm glad there's someone else in this house who flies into the same rages as I do. Peter seemed relieved that he could criticize Dussel without being afraid I'd tell. As for me, I was pleased too, because I sensed a strong feeling of fellowship, which I only remember having had with my girlfriends.

Yours, Anne

The minor run-in with Dussel had several repercussions, for which he had only himself to blame. Monday evening Dussel came in to see Mother and told her triumphantly that Peter had asked him that morning if he'd slept well, and then added how sorry he was about what had happened Sunday evening – he hadn't really meant what he'd said. Dussel assured him he hadn't taken it to heart. So everything was right as rain again. Mother passed this story on to me, and I was secretly amazed that Peter, who'd been so angry with Dussel, had humbled himself, despite all his assurances to the contrary.

I couldn't refrain from sounding Peter out on the subject, and he instantly replied that Dussel had been lying. You should have seen Peter's face. I wish I'd had a camera. Indignation, rage, indecision, agitation and much more crossed his face in rapid succession.

That evening Mr van Daan and Peter really told Dussel off. But it couldn't have been all that bad, since Peter had another dental appointment today.

Actually, they never wanted to speak to each other again.

Peter and I hadn't talked to each other all day, except for a few meaningless words. It was too cold to go up to the attic, and anyway, it was Margot's birthday. At twelve-thirty he came to look at the presents and hung around chatting longer than was strictly necessary, something he'd never have done otherwise. But I got my chance in the afternoon. Since I felt like spoiling Margot on her birthday, I went to get the coffee, and after that the potatoes. When I came to Peter's room, he immediately took his papers off the stairs, and I asked if I should close the trapdoor to the attic.

'Yes,' he said, 'go ahead. When you're ready to come back down, just knock and I'll open it for you.'

I thanked him, went upstairs and spent at least ten minutes searching around in the barrel for the smallest potatoes. My back started aching, and the attic was cold. Naturally, I didn't bother to knock but opened the trapdoor myself. But he obligingly got up and took the pan out of my hands.

'I did my best, but I couldn't find any smaller ones.'

'Did you look in the big barrel?'

'Yes, I've been through them all.'

By this time I was at the bottom of the stairs, and he examined the pan of potatoes he was still holding. 'Oh, but these are fine,' he said, and added, as I took the pan from him, 'My compliments!'

As he said this, he gave me such a warm, tender look that I started glowing inside. I could tell he wanted to please me, but since he couldn't make a long complimentary speech, he said everything with his eyes. I understood him so well and was very grateful. It still makes me happy to think back to those words and that look!

When I went downstairs, Mother said she needed more potatoes, this time for dinner, so I volunteered to go back up. When I entered Peter's room, I apologized for disturbing him again. As I was going up the stairs, he stood up, went over to stand between the stairs and the wall, grabbed my arm and tried to stop me.

'I'll go,' he said. 'I have to go upstairs anyway.'

I replied that it wasn't really necessary, that I didn't have to get only the small ones this time. Convinced, he let go of my arm. On my way back, he opened the trapdoor and once again took the pan from me. Standing by the door, I asked, 'What are you working on?'

'French,' he replied.

I asked if I could take a look at his lessons. Then I went to wash my hands and sat down across from him on the divan.

After I'd explained some French to him, we began to talk. He told me that after the war he wanted to go to the Dutch East Indies and live on a rubber plantation. He talked about his life at home, the black market and what a hopeless case he is. I told him he had a big inferiority complex. He talked about the war, saying that Russia and England were bound to go to war against each other, and about the Jews. He said life would have been much easier if he'd been a Christian or could become one after the war. I asked if he wanted to be baptized, but that wasn't what he meant either. He said he'd never be able to feel like a Christian, but that after the war he'd make sure nobody would know he was Jewish. I felt a momentary pang. It's such a shame he still has a touch of dishonesty in him.

Peter added, 'The Jews have been and always will be the chosen people!'

I answered, 'Just this once, I hope they'll be chosen for something good!'

But we went on chatting very pleasantly, about Father, about judging human character and all sorts of things, so many that I can't even remember them all.

I left at a quarter past five, because Bep had arrived.

That evening he said something else I thought was nice. We were talking about the picture of a film star I'd once given him, which has been hanging in his room for at least a year and a half. He liked it so much that I offered to give him a few more.

'No,' he replied, 'I'd rather keep the one I've got. I look at it every day, and the people in it have become my friends.'

I now have a better understanding of why he always hugs Mouschi so tightly. He obviously needs affection too. I forgot to mention something else he was talking about. He said, 'No, I'm not afraid, except when it comes to things about myself, but I'm working on that.'

Peter has a huge inferiority complex. For example, he always thinks he's so stupid and we're so clever. When I help him with French, he thanks me a thousand times. One of these days I'm going to say, 'Oh, cut it out! You're much better at English and geography!'

Anne Frank

THURSDAY, 17 FEBRUARY 1944

Dear Kitty,

I was upstairs this morning, since I promised Mrs van D. I'd read her some of my stories. I began with 'Eva's Dream', which she liked a lot, and then I read a few passages from 'The Secret Annexe', which had her in stitches. Peter also listened for a while (just the last part) and asked if I'd come to his room sometime to read more. I decided I had to take a chance right then and there, so I got my exercise-book and let him read that bit where Cady and Hans talk about God. I can't really tell what kind of impression it made on him. He said something I don't quite remember, not about whether it was good, but about the idea behind it. I told him I just wanted him to see that I didn't write only amusing things. He nodded, and I left the room. We'll see if I hear anything more!

Yours, Anne Frank

My dearest Kitty,

Whenever I go upstairs, it's always so I can see 'him'. Now that I have something to look forward to, my life here has improved greatly.

At least the object of my friendship is always here, and I don't have to be afraid of rivals (except for Margot). Don't think I'm in love, because I'm not, but I do have the feeling that something beautiful is going to develop between Peter and me, a kind of friendship and a feeling of trust. I go and see him whenever I get the chance, and it's not the way it used to be, when he didn't know what to make of me. On the contrary, he's still talking away as I'm heading out of the door. Mother doesn't like me going upstairs. She always says I'm bothering Peter and that I should leave him alone. Honestly, can't she credit me with some intuition? She always looks at me so oddly when I go to Peter's room. When I come down again, she asks me where I've been. It's terrible, but I'm beginning to hate her!

Yours, Anne M. Frank

Dearest Kitty,

It's Saturday again, and that should tell you enough. This morning all was quiet. I spent nearly an hour upstairs making meatballs, but I only spoke to 'him' in passing.

When everyone went upstairs at two-thirty to either read or take a nap, I went downstairs, with blanket and all, to sit at the desk and read or write. Before long I couldn't take it any more. I put my head in my arms and sobbed my heart out. The tears streamed down my cheeks, and I felt desperately unhappy. Oh, if only 'he' had come to comfort me.

It was past four by the time I went upstairs again. At five o'clock I set off to get some potatoes, hoping once again that we'd meet, but while I was still in the bathroom fixing my hair, he went to see Boche.

I wanted to help Mrs van D. and went upstairs with my book and everything, but suddenly I felt the tears coming back. I raced downstairs to the lavatory, grabbing the mirror on the way. I sat there on the toilet, fully dressed, long after I was through, my tears leaving dark spots on the red of my apron, and I felt utterly dejected.

Here's what was going through my mind: 'Oh, I'll never reach Peter this way. Who knows, maybe he doesn't even like me and he doesn't need anyone to confide in. Maybe he only thinks of me in a casual sort of way. I'll have to go back to being alone, without anyone to confide in and without Peter, without hope, comfort or anything to look forward to. Oh, if only I could rest my head on his shoulder and not feel so hopelessly alone and deserted! Who knows, maybe he doesn't care for me at all and looks at the others in the same tender way. Maybe I only imagined it was especially for me. Oh, Peter, if only you could hear me or see me. If the truth is disappointing, I won't be able to bear it.'

A little later I felt hopeful and full of expectation again, though my tears were still flowing – on the inside.

Yours, Anne M. Frank

But how and when will we finally reach each other?

I don't know how much longer I can continue to keep this yearning under control.

Yours, Anne M. Frank

My dearest Kitty,

It's like a nightmare, one that goes on long after I'm awake. I see him nearly every hour of the day and yet I can't be with him, I can't let the others notice, and I have to pretend to be cheerful, though my heart is aching.

Peter Schiff and Peter van Daan have melted into one Peter, who's good and kind and whom I long for desperately. Mother's horrible, Father's nice, which makes him even more exasperating, and Margot's the worst, since she takes advantage of my smiling face to claim me for herself, when all I want is to be left alone.

Peter didn't join me in the attic, but went up to the loft to do some carpentry work. At every rasp and bang, another chunk of my courage broke off and I was even more unhappy. In the distance a clock was tolling 'Be pure in heart, be pure in mind!'

I'm sentimental, I know. I'm despondent and foolish, I know that too.

Oh, help me!

Yours, Anne M. Frank

Dearest Kitty,

My own affairs have been pushed to the background by ... a break-in. I'm boring you with all my break-ins, but what can I do when burglars take such pleasure in honouring Gies & Co. with their presence? This incident is much more complicated than the last one, in July 1943.

Last night at seven-thirty Mr van Daan was heading, as usual, for Mr Kugler's office when he saw that both the glass door and the office door were open. He was surprised, but he went on through and was even more astonished to see that the alcove doors were open as well and that there was a terrible mess in the front office. 'There's been a burglary' flashed through his mind. But just to make sure, he went downstairs to the front door, checked the lock and found everything closed. 'Bep and Peter must just have been very careless this evening,' Mr van D. concluded. He remained for a while in Mr Kugler's office, switched off the lamp and went upstairs without worrying much about the open doors or the messy office.

Early this morning Peter knocked at our door to tell us that the front door was wide open and that the projector and Mr Kugler's new briefcase had disappeared from the cupboard. Peter was instructed to lock the door. Mr van Daan told us about his discoveries of the night before, and we were extremely worried.

The only explanation is that the burglar must have had a duplicate key, since there were no signs of a forced entry. He must have sneaked in early in the evening, shut the door behind him, hidden himself when he heard Mr van Daan, fled with the loot after Mr van Daan went upstairs and, in his hurry, not bothered to shut the door.

Who could have our key? Why didn't the burglar go to the warehouse? Was it one of our own warehouse employees, and will he turn us in, now that he's heard Mr van Daan and maybe even seen him?

It's really scary, since we don't know whether the burglar will take it into his head to try and get in again. Or was he so startled when he heard someone else in the building that he'll stay away?

Yours, Anne

PS. We'd be delighted if you could search out a good detective for us. Obviously, there's one condition: he must be relied upon not to inform on people in hiding.

THURSDAY, 2 MARCH 1944

Dearest Kitty,

Margot and I were in the attic together today. I can't enjoy being there with her the way I imagine it'd be with Peter (or someone else). I know she feels the same about most things as I do!

While washing up, Bep began talking to Mother and Mrs van Daan about how discouraged she gets. What help did those two offer her? Our tactless mother, especially, only made things go from bad to worse. Do you know what her advice was? That she should think about all the other people in the world who are suffering! How can thinking about the misery of others help if you're miserable yourself? I said as much. Their response, of course, was that I should stay out of conversations of this sort.

The grown-ups are such idiots! As if Peter, Margot, Bep and I didn't all have the same feelings. The only thing that helps is a mother's love, or that of a very, very close friend. But these two mothers don't understand the first thing about us! Perhaps Mrs van Daan does, a bit more than Mother. Oh, I wish I could have said something to poor Bep, something that I know from my own experience would have helped. But Father came between us, pushing me roughly aside. They're all so stupid!

I also talked to Margot about Father and Mother, about how nice it could be here if they weren't so aggravating. We'd be able to organize evenings in which everyone could take turns discussing a given subject. But we've already been through all that. It's impossible for me to talk here! Mr van Daan goes on the offensive, Mother gets sarcastic and can't say *anything* in a normal voice, Father doesn't feel like taking part, nor does Mr Dussel, and Mrs van D. is attacked so often that she just sits there with a red face, hardly able to put up a fight any more. And what about us? We aren't allowed to have an opinion! My, my, aren't they progressive! Not have an opinion! People can tell you to shut up, but they can't keep you from having an opinion. You can't forbid someone to have an opinion, no matter how young they are! The only thing that would help Bep, Margot, Peter and me would be great love and devotion, which we don't get here. And no one, especially not the idiotic sages around here, is capable of understanding us, since we're more sensitive and much more advanced in our thinking than any of them ever suspect!

Love, what is love? I don't think you can really put it into words. Love is understanding someone, caring for him, sharing his joys and sorrows. This eventually includes physical love. You've shared something, given something away and received something in return, whether or not you're married, whether or not you have a baby. Losing your virtue doesn't matter, as long as you know that for as long as you live you'll have someone at your side who understands you, and who doesn't have to be shared with anyone else!

Yours, Anne M. Frank

At the moment, Mother's grumbling at me again; she's clearly jealous because I talk to Mrs van Daan more than to her. What do I care!

I managed to get hold of Peter this afternoon, and we talked for at least forty-five minutes. He wanted to tell me something about himself, but didn't find it easy. He finally got it out, though it took a long time. I honestly didn't know whether it was better for me to stay or to go. But I wanted so much to help him! I told him about Bep and how tactless our mothers are. He told me that his parents argue constantly, about politics and cigarettes and all kinds of things. As I've told you before, Peter's very shy, but not too shy to admit that he'd be perfectly happy not to see his parents for a year or two. 'My father isn't as nice as he looks,' he said. 'But in the matter of the cigarettes, Mother's absolutely right.'

I also told him about my mother. But he came to Father's defence. He thought he was a 'terrific chap'.

Tonight when I was hanging up my apron after washing up, he called me over and asked me not to say anything downstairs about his parents' having had another argument and not being on speaking terms. I promised, though I'd already told Margot. But I'm sure Margot won't pass it on.

'Oh no, Peter,' I said, 'you don't have to worry about me. I've learned not to blab everything I hear. I never repeat what you tell me.'

He was glad to hear that. I also told him what terrible gossips we are, and said, 'Margot's quite right, of course, when she says I'm not being honest, because as much as I want to stop gossiping, there's nothing I like better than discussing Mr Dussel.'

'It's good that you admit it,' he said. He blushed, and his sincere compliment almost embarrassed me too.

Then we talked about 'upstairs' and 'downstairs' some more. Peter was really rather surprised to hear that we don't like his parents. 'Peter,' I said, 'you know I'm always honest, so why shouldn't I tell you this as well? We can see their faults too.'

I added, 'Peter, I'd really like to help you. Will you let me? You're caught in an awkward position, and I know, even though you don't say anything, that it upsets you.'

'Oh, your help is always welcome!'

'Maybe it'd be better for you to talk to Father. You can tell him anything, he won't pass it on.'

'I know, he's a real pal.'

'You like him a lot, don't you?'

Peter nodded, and I continued, 'Well, he likes you too, you know!'

He looked up quickly and blushed. It was really touching to see how happy these few words made him. 'You think so?' he asked.

'Yes,' I said. 'You can tell from the little things he lets slip now and then.'

Then Mr van Daan came in to do some dictating. Peter's a 'terrific chap', just like Father!

Yours, Anne M. Frank

FRIDAY, 3 MARCH 1944

My dearest Kitty,

When I looked into the candle tonight, I felt calm and happy again. It seems Grandma is in that candle, and it's

Grandma who watches over and protects me and makes me feel happy again. But . . . there's someone else who governs all my moods and that's . . . Peter. I went to get the potatoes today, and while I was standing on the stairway with my pan full, he asked, 'What did you do during lunch break?'

I sat down on the stairs, and we began to talk. The potatoes didn't make it to the kitchen until five-fifteen (an hour after I'd gone to get them). Peter didn't say anything more about his parents; we just talked about books and about the past. Oh, he gazes at me with such warmth in his eyes; I don't think it will take much for me to fall in love with him.

He brought the subject up this evening. I went to his room after peeling potatoes and remarked on how hot it was. 'You can tell the temperature by looking at Margot and me, because we turn white when it's cold and red when it's hot,' I said.

'In love?' he asked.

'Why should I be in love?' It was a pretty silly answer (or, rather, question).

'Why not?' he said, and then it was time for dinner.

What did he mean? Today I finally managed to ask him whether my chatter bothered him. All he said was, 'Oh, it's fine with me!' I can't tell how much of his reply was due to shyness.

Kitty, I sound like someone who's in love and can talk about nothing but her dearest darling. And Peter is a darling. Will I ever be able to tell him that? Only if he thinks the same of me, but I'm the kind of person you have to treat with kid gloves, I know that all too well. And he likes to be left alone, so I don't know how much he likes me. In any case, we're getting to know each other a little better. I wish we dared to say more. But who knows, maybe that time will come sooner than I think! Once or twice a day he gives me a knowing glance, I wink back, and we're both happy. It seems insane to talk about his being happy, and yet I have the overwhelming feeling he thinks the same way I do.

Yours, Anne M. Frank

Dear Kitty,

This is the first Saturday in months that hasn't been tiresome, dreary and boring. The reason is Peter. This morning as I was on my way to the attic to hang up my apron, Father asked whether I wanted to stay and practise my French, and I said yes. We spoke French together for a while and I explained something to Peter, and then we worked on our English. Father read aloud from Dickens, and I was in seventh heaven, since I was sitting on Father's chair, close to Peter.

I went downstairs at quarter to eleven. When I went back up at eleven-thirty, Peter was already waiting for me on the stairs. We talked until quarter to one. Whenever I leave the room, for example after a meal, and Peter has a chance and no one else can hear, he says, 'Cheerio, Anne, see you later.'

Oh, I'm so happy! I wonder if he's going to fall in love with me after all? In any case, he's a nice boy, and you have no idea how good it is to talk to him!

Mrs van D. thinks it's all right for me to talk to Peter, but today she asked me teasingly, 'Can I trust you two up there?'

'Of course,' I protested. 'I take that as an insult!' Morning, noon and night, I look forward to seeing Peter.

Yours, Anne M. Frank

PS. Before I forget, last night everything was blanketed in snow. Now it's thawed and there's almost nothing left.

Dearest Kitty,

Ever since Peter told me about his parents, I've felt a certain sense of responsibility towards him – don't you think that's strange? It's as though their quarrels were just as much my business as his, and yet I don't dare bring it up any more, because I'm afraid it makes him uncomfortable. I wouldn't want to intrude, not for all the money in the world.

I can tell by Peter's face that he ponders things just as deeply as I do. Last night I was annoyed when Mrs van D. scoffed, 'The thinker!' Peter flushed and looked embarrassed, and I nearly blew my top.

Why don't these people keep their mouths shut? You can't imagine what it's like to have to stand on the sidelines and see how lonely he is, without being able to do anything. I can imagine, as if I were in his place, how despondent he must sometimes feel at the quarrels. And about love. Poor Peter, he needs to be loved so much!

It sounded so cold when he said he didn't need any friends. Oh, he's so wrong! I don't think he means it. He clings to his masculinity, his solitude and his feigned indifference so he can maintain his role, so he'll never, ever have to show his feelings. Poor Peter, how long can he keep it up? Won't he explode from this superhuman effort?

Oh, Peter, if only I could help you, if only you would let me! Together we could banish our loneliness, yours and mine!

I've been doing a great deal of thinking, but not saying much. I'm happy when I see him, and happier still if the sun shines when we're together. I washed my hair yesterday, and because I knew he was next door, I was very rambunctious. I couldn't help it; the more quiet and serious I am on the inside, the noisier I get on the outside! Who will be the first to discover the chink in my armour?

It's just as well that the van Daans don't have a daughter. My conquest could never be so challenging, so beautiful and so nice with someone of the same sex!

Yours, Anne M. Frank

PS. You know I'm always honest with you, so I think I should tell you that I live from one encounter to the next. I keep hoping to discover that he's dying to see me, and I'm in raptures when I notice his bashful attempts. I think he'd like to be able to express himself as easily as I do; little does he know it's his awkwardness that I find so touching.

TUESDAY, 7 MARCH 1944

Dearest Kitty,

When I think back to my life in 1942, it all seems so unreal. The Anne Frank who enjoyed that heavenly existence was completely different from the one who has grown wise within these walls. Yes, it was heavenly. Five admirers on every street corner, twenty or so friends, the favourite of most of my teachers, spoiled rotten by Father and Mother, bags full of sweets and loads of pocket money. What more could anyone ask for?

You're probably wondering how I could have charmed all those people. Peter says it's because I'm 'attractive', but that isn't it entirely. The teachers were amused and entertained by my clever answers, my witty remarks, my smiling face and my critical mind. That's all I was: a terrible flirt, coquettish and amusing. I had a few plus points, which kept me in everybody's good graces: I was hardworking, honest and generous. I would never have refused anyone who wanted to peek at my answers, I was magnanimous with my sweets, and I wasn't stuck-up.

Would all that admiration eventually have made me over-confident? It's a good thing that, at the height of my glory, I was suddenly plunged into reality. It took me more than a year to get used to doing without admiration.

How did they see me at school? As the class comedian, the eternal ringleader, never in a bad mood, never a cry-baby. Was it any wonder that everyone wanted to cycle to school with me or do me little favours?

I look back at that Anne Frank as a pleasant, amusing, but superficial girl, who has nothing to do with me. What did Peter say about me? 'Whenever I saw you, you were surrounded by a flock of girls and at least two boys, you were always laughing, and you were always the centre of attention!' He was right.

What's remained of that Anne Frank? Oh, I haven't forgotten how to laugh or toss off a remark, I'm just as good, if not better, at hauling people over the coals, and I can still flirt and be amusing, if I want to be . . .

But there's the catch. I'd like to live that seemingly carefree and happy life for an evening, a few days, a week. At the end of that week I'd be exhausted, and would be grateful to the first person to talk to me about something meaningful. I want friends, not admirers. People who respect me for my character and my deeds, not my flattering smile. The circle around me would be much smaller, but what does that matter, as long as they're sincere?

In spite of everything, I wasn't altogether happy in 1942; I often felt I'd been deserted, but because I was on the go all day long, I didn't think about it. I enjoyed myself as much as I could, trying consciously or unconsciously to fill the void with jokes.

Looking back, I realize that this period of my life has irrevocably come to a close; my happy-go-lucky, carefree schooldays are gone for ever. I don't even miss them. I've outgrown them. I can no longer just be frivolous, since my serious side is always there.

I see my life up till New Year 1944 as if I were looking through a powerful magnifying glass. When I was at home, my life was filled with sunshine. Then, in the middle of 1942, everything changed overnight. The quarrels, the accusations – I couldn't take it all in. I was caught off guard, and the only way I knew how to keep my bearings was to talk back.

The first half of 1943 brought crying spells, loneliness and the gradual realization of my faults and shortcomings, which were numerous and seemed even more so. I filled the day with chatter, tried to draw Pim closer to me and failed. This left me on my own to face the difficult task of improving myself so I wouldn't have to hear their reproaches, because they made me so despondent.

The second half of the year was slightly better. I became a teenager, and was treated more like a grown-up. I began to think about things and to write stories, finally coming to the conclusion that the others no longer had anything to do with me. They had no right to swing me back and forth like a pendulum on a clock. I wanted to change myself in my own way. I realized I could manage without my mother, completely and totally, and that hurt. But what affected me even more was the realization that I was never going to be able to confide in Father. I didn't trust anyone but myself.

After New Year the second big change occurred: my dream, through which I discovered my longing for . . . a boy; not for a girlfriend, but for a boyfriend. I also discovered an inner happiness underneath my superficial and cheerful exterior. From time to time I was quiet. Now I live only for Peter, since what happens to me in the future depends largely on him!

I lie in bed at night, after ending my prayers with the words *'Ich danke dir für all das Gute und Liebe und Schöne'*,* and I'm filled with joy. I think of going into hiding, my health and my whole being as *das Gute*; Peter's love (which is still so new and fragile and which neither of us dares to say aloud), the future, happiness and love as *das Liebe*; the world, nature and the tremendous beauty of everything, all that splendour, as *das Schöne*.

At such moments I don't think about all the misery, but about the beauty that still remains. This is where Mother and I differ greatly. Her advice in the face of melancholy is: 'Think about all the suffering in the world and be thankful you're not part of it.' My advice is: 'Go outside, to the country, enjoy the sun and all nature has to offer. Go outside and try to recapture the happiness within yourself; think of all the beauty in yourself and in everything around you and be happy.'

I don't think Mother's advice can be right, because what are you supposed to do if you become part of the suffering? You'd be completely lost. On the contrary, beauty remains, even in misfortune. If you just look for it, you discover more and more happiness and regain your balance. A person who's happy will make others happy; a person who has courage and faith will never die in misery!

Yours, Anne M. Frank

---

* Thank you, God, for all that is good and dear and beautiful.

Margot and I have been writing each other notes, just for fun, of course.

Anne: It's strange, but I can only remember the day after what has happened the night before. For example, I suddenly remembered that Mr Dussel was snoring loudly last night. (It's now quarter to three on Wednesday afternoon and Mr Dussel is snoring again, which is why it flashed through my mind, of course.) When I had to use the potty, I deliberately made more noise to get the snoring to stop.

Margot: Which is better, the snoring or the gasping for air?

Anne: The snoring's better, because it stops when I make a noise, without waking the person in question.

What I didn't write to Margot, but what I'll confess to you, dear Kitty, is that I've been dreaming of Peter a great deal. The night before last I dreamed I was skating right here in our living-room with that little boy from the Apollo skating-rink; he was with his sister, the girl with the spindly legs who always wore the same blue dress. I introduced myself, overdoing it a bit, and asked him his name. It was Peter. In my dream I wondered just how many Peters I actually knew!

Then I dreamed we were standing in Peter's room, facing each other beside the stairs. I said something to him; he gave me a kiss, but replied that he didn't love me all that much and that I shouldn't flirt. In a desperate and pleading voice I said, 'I'm not flirting, Peter!'

When I woke up, I was glad Peter hasn't said it after all.

Last night I dreamed we were kissing each other, but Peter's cheeks were very disappointing: they weren't as soft as they looked. They were more like Father's cheeks – the cheeks of a man who already shaves.

My dearest Kitty,

The proverb 'Misfortunes never come singly' definitely applies to today. Peter just said so. Let me tell you all the awful things that have happened and that are still hanging over our heads.

First, Miep is ill, as a result of Henk and Aagje's wedding yesterday. She caught a cold in the Westerkerk, where the service was held. Second, Mr Kleiman hasn't returned to work since the last time his stomach started bleeding, so Bep's been left to hold the fort alone. Third, the police have arrested a man (whose name I won't put in writing). It's terrible not only for him, but for us as well, since he's been supplying us with potatoes, butter and jam. Mr M., as I'll call him, has five children under the age of thirteen, and another on the way.

Last night we had another little scare: we were in the middle of dinner when suddenly someone knocked on the wall next door. For the rest of the evening we were nervous and gloomy.

Lately I haven't been at all in the mood to write down what's been going on here. I've been more wrapped up in myself. Don't get me wrong, I'm terribly upset about what's happened to poor, good-hearted Mr M., but there's not much room for him in my diary.

Tuesday, Wednesday and Thursday I was in Peter's room from four-thirty to five-fifteen. We worked on our French and chatted about one thing and another. I really look forward to that hour or so in the afternoon, but best of all is that I think Peter's just as pleased to see me.

Yours, Anne M. Frank

SATURDAY, 11 MARCH 1944

Dearest Kitty,

I haven't been able to sit still lately. I wander upstairs and down and then back again. I like talking to Peter, but I'm always afraid of being a nuisance. He's told me a bit about the past, about his parents and about himself, but it's not enough, and every five minutes I wonder why I find myself longing for more. He used to think I was a real pain in the neck, and the feeling was mutual. I've changed my mind, but how do I know he's changed his? I think he has, but that doesn't necessarily mean we have to become the best of friends, although as far as I'm concerned, it would make our time here more bearable. But I won't let this drive me crazy. I spend enough time thinking about him and don't have to get you worked up as well, simply because I'm so miserable!

SUNDAY, 12 MARCH 1944

Dearest Kitty,

Things are getting crazier here as the days go by. Peter hasn't looked at me since yesterday. He's been behaving as if he's cross with me. I'm doing my best not to chase after him and to talk to him as little as possible, but it's not easy! What's going on, what makes him keep me at arm's length one minute and rush back to my side the next? Perhaps I'm imagining that it's worse than it really is. Perhaps he's just moody like me, and tomorrow everything will be all right again!

I have the hardest time trying to maintain a normal façade when I'm feeling so wretched and sad. I have to talk, help around the house, sit with the others and, above all, act cheerful! Most of all I miss the outdoors and having a place where I can be alone for as long as I want! I think I'm getting everything all mixed up, Kitty, but then, I'm in a state of utter confusion: on the one hand, I'm half mad with desire for him, can hardly be in the same room without looking at him; and on the other hand, I wonder why he should matter to me so much and why I can't be calm again!

Day and night, during every waking hour, I do nothing but ask myself, 'Have you given him enough chance to be alone? Have you been spending too much time upstairs? Do you talk too much about serious subjects he's not yet ready to talk about? Maybe he doesn't even like you? Has it all been your imagination? But then why has he told you so much about himself? Is he sorry he did?' And a whole lot more.

Yesterday afternoon I was so worn out by the sad news from the outside that I lay down on my divan for a nap. All I wanted was to sleep and not have to think. I slept until four, but then I had to go next door. It wasn't easy, answering all Mother's questions and inventing an excuse to explain my nap to Father. I pleaded a headache, which wasn't a lie, since I did have one . . . on the inside!

Ordinary people, ordinary girls, teenagers like myself, would think all this self-pity is a little crazy. But that's just it. I pour my heart out to you, and the rest of the time I'm as impudent, cheerful and self-confident as possible to avoid questions and keep from getting on my own nerves.

Margot is very kind and would like me to confide in her,

but I can't tell her everything. She takes me too seriously, far too seriously, and spends a lot of time thinking about her loony sister, looking at me closely whenever I open my mouth and wondering, 'Is she acting, or does she really mean it?'

It's because we're always together. I don't want the person I confide in to be around me all the time.

When will I untangle my jumbled thoughts? When will I find inner peace again?

Yours, Anne

TUESDAY, 14 MARCH 1944

Dearest Kitty,

It might be amusing for you (though not for me) to hear what we're going to eat today. The cleaning lady is working downstairs, so at the moment I'm seated at the van Daans' oilcloth-covered table with a handkerchief sprinkled with fragrant pre-war perfume pressed to my nose and mouth. You probably don't have the faintest idea what I'm talking about, so let me 'begin at the beginning'. The people who supply us with food coupons have been arrested, so we have just our five black-market ration books – no coupons, no fats and oils. Since Miep and Mr Kleiman are ill again, Bep can't manage the shopping. The food is wretched, and so are we. As of tomorrow, we won't have a scrap of fat, butter or margarine. We can't eat fried potatoes for breakfast (which we've been doing to save on bread), so we're having porridge instead, and because Mrs van D. thinks we're starving, we bought some milk and some cream. Lunch today consists of mashed potatoes and pickled kale. This explains the precautionary measure with the handkerchief. You wouldn't believe how much kale can stink when it's a few years old! The kitchen smells like a mixture of spoiled plums, rotten eggs and brine. Ugh, just the thought of having to eat that muck makes me want to be sick! Besides that, our potatoes have contracted such strange diseases that one out of every two buckets of *pommes de terre* ends up in the dustbin. We entertain ourselves by trying to work out which disease they've got, and we've reached the conclusion that they suffer from cancer, smallpox and measles. Honestly, being in hiding during the fourth year of the war is no picnic. If only the whole stinking mess were over!

To tell you the truth, the food wouldn't matter so much to me if life here were more pleasant in other ways. But that's just it: this tedious existence is starting to make us all disagreeable. Here are the opinions of the five grown-ups on the present situation (children aren't allowed to have opinions, and for once I'm sticking to the rules):

Mrs van Daan: 'I'd stopped wanting to be queen of the kitchen long ago. But sitting around doing nothing was boring, so I went back to cooking. Still, I can't help complaining: it's impossible to cook without oil, and all those disgusting smells make me feel like retching. Besides, what do I get in return for my efforts? Ingratitude and rude remarks. I'm always the black sheep; I get blamed for everything. What's more, it's my opinion that the war is making very little progress. The Germans will win in the end. I'm terrified that we're going to starve, and when I'm in a bad mood, I snap at everyone who comes near.'

Mr van Daan: 'I just smoke and smoke and smoke. Then the food, the political situation and Kerli's moods don't seem so bad. Kerli's a sweetheart. If I don't have anything to smoke, I feel ill, then I need to eat meat, life becomes unbearable, nothing's good enough, and there's bound to be a flaming row. My Kerli's an idiot.'

Mrs Frank: 'Food's not very important, but I'd love a slice

of rye bread right now, because I'm so hungry. If I were Mrs van Daan, I'd have put a stop to Mr van Daan's smoking long ago. But I desperately need a cigarette now, because my head's in such a whirl. The van Daans are horrible people; the British may make a lot of mistakes, but the war is progressing. I should keep my mouth shut and be grateful I'm not in Poland.'

Mr Frank: 'Everything's fine, I don't need a thing. Stay calm, we've got plenty of time. Just give me my potatoes, and I'll be quiet. Better set aside some of my rations for Bep. The political situation is improving, I'm extremely optimistic.'

Mr Dussel: 'I must complete the task I've set for myself, everything must be finished on time. The political situation is looking "*gut*", it's "eempossible" for us to get caught. Me, me, me . . . !'

Yours, Anne

THURSDAY, 16 MARCH 1944

Dearest Kitty,

Whew! Released from the gloom and doom for a few moments! All I've been hearing today is: 'If this and that happens, we're in trouble, and if so-and-so falls ill, we'll be left to fend for ourselves, and if . . .'

Well, you know the rest, or at any rate I assume you're familiar enough with the residents of the Annexe to guess what they'd be talking about.

The reason for all the 'ifs' is that Mr Kugler has been called up for a six-day work detail, Bep is down with a bad cold and will probably have to stay home tomorrow, Miep hasn't got over her flu, and Mr Kleiman's stomach bled so much he lost consciousness. What a tale of woe!

We think Mr Kugler should go directly to a reliable doctor